1987

THE CRITICS DEBATE

General Editor Michael Scott

The Critics Debate
General Editor Michael Scott
Published titles:
Sons and Lovers Geoffrey Harvey
Bleak House Jeremy Hawthorn
The Canterbury Tales Alcuin Blamires
Tess of the d'Urbervilles Terence Wright

Further titles are in preparation.

THE
CANTERBURY TALES

Alcuin Blamires

HUMANITIES PRESS INTERNATIONAL, INC.
Atlantic Highlands, NJ

First published in 1987 in the United States of America by HUMANITIE
PRESS INTERNATIONAL, INC., Atlantic Highlands, NJ 07716

Library of Congress Cataloging-in-Publication Data

Blamires, Alcuin.
  The Canterbury tales.

  (The Critics debate)
  Bibliography: p.
  Includes indexes.
  1. Chaucer, Geoffrey, *d. 1400*. Canterbury tales
I. Title II. Series
PR1874.B58 1987 821'.1 86-7441

ISBN 0–391–03449–9
ISBN 0–391–03444–8 (Pbk.)

PRINTED IN HONG KONG

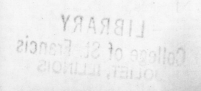

Contents

General Editor's Preface

OVER THE last few years the practice of literary criticism has become hotly debated. Methods developed earlier in the century and before have been attacked and the word 'crisis' has been drawn upon to describe the present condition of English Studies. That such a debate is taking place is a sign of the subject discipline's health. Some would hold that the situation necessitates a radical alternative approach which naturally implies a 'crisis situation'. Others would respond that to employ such terms is to precipitate or construct a false position. The debate continues but it is not the first. 'New Criticism' acquired its title because it attempted something fresh calling into question certain practices of the past. Yet the practices it attacked were not entirely lost or negated by the new critics. One factor becomes clear: English Studies is a pluralistic discipline.

What are students coming to advanced work in English for the first time to make of all this debate and controversy? They are in danger of being overwhelmed by the cross currents of critical approaches as they take up their study of literature. The purpose of this series is to help delineate various critical approaches to specific literary texts. Its authors are from a variety of critical schools and have approached their task in a flexible manner. Their aim is to help the reader come to terms with the variety of criticism and to introduce him or her to further reading on the subject and to a fuller evaluation of a particular text by illustrating the way it has been approached in a number of contexts. In the first part of the book a critical survey is given of some of the major ways the text has been appraised. This is done sometimes in a thematic manner, sometimes according to various 'schools' or 'approaches'. In the second part the authors provide their own appraisals of the text from their stated critical standpoint, allowing the reader the knowledge of their own particular approaches from which their views may in turn be evaluated. The series therein hopes to introduce and to elucidate criticism of authors and texts being studied and to encourage participation as the critics debate.

Michael Scott

A Note on Text and References

THE TEXT used here derives from *The Works of Geoffrey Chaucer*, edited by F. N. Robinson, second edition (London, 1957). Line-numbering in the *Tales* is as allocated by Robinson within his division of the poem's fragments according to Roman numerals. The reader working from an individual edition of a tale (e.g. one of those published by Cambridge University Press) should note that there will possibly be unavoidable discrepancies between the line-numbering in that edition, and the numbering adopted from Robinson in this book. Line references appear in square brackets.

Other references are given in round brackets. Critical works discussed are cited by author and date of publication, with page references as appropriate. From the name and date, the reader can locate the relevant publication in the References at the end. In cases where the critic named in a given section does not appear in the corresponding section of the References, consult the Index. It is quite in order for those using this volume as a handbook on the general picture of *Tales* criticism, to develop an immunity against secondary references.

For quotations from medieval sources other than Chaucer, the editions used are as specified in the last section of the References.

Part One
Survey

Introduction

CHAUCER scholars are not noted for the speed with which they absorb the latest literary theory. One contributor to a volume entitled *New Perspectives in Chaucer Criticism* remarked that 'just as it was some fifteen years before New Criticism [i.e. "close reading"] reached Chaucer in the 1950s, so it is the case with new literary theorizing, which is now about ripe to reach Chaucer' (Bloomfield 1981, p.25). Poised at this moment of somewhat nervous anticipation, Bloomfield settled for an inspection of recent theoretical positions themselves, lining them up like suspects in a police identification parade and speculating which theory might be expected to yield positive results in relation to Chaucer.

Since then the threshold has been crossed. As we shall see, certain explorations of *The Canterbury Tales* are beginning to apply the tenets of post-modern theory. On the face of it, indeed, Chaucer's poetry constitutes ground that is wide open to some streams of contemporary theory. If, for example, in some quarters the capacity of an author to exercise authority over the meaning of what he writes is now considered doubtful, we may observe that Chaucer is uneasy about literary authority and so self-conscious about his own authorship that he keeps on minimising his responsibility for his narratives. If, again, the concept of an innocent or passive or objective reader is now widely held to be a pipe-dream, we may notice how the Canterbury pilgrims themselves (who are in a sense the first 'readers' of the various tales) lack objectivity. They are conspicuously liable to engage with each other's stories in blinkered, self-oriented ways. In this connection it is interesting to see what happens in an earlier poem, *The Parliament of Fowls*, when Chaucer represents himself in the act of reading a book. The book is an austere commentary by Macrobius on man's place in the cosmos, and it seems to dissatisfy the love-poet: 'For bothe I hadde thyng which that I nolde, / And ek I nadde that thyng that I wolde' [90–1]. Macrobius gave him what he didn't want (that is, commendations of selfless human

1

fellowship), and didn't give him what he wanted (apparently, insight into romantic love). In one way this looks critically archaic because the book is read for whatever 'thing' or lump of 'message' it can convey. But Chaucer's wry admission of his frustration (among other functions it has) also anticipates modern assertions that readers are not empty receptacles, but bring highly active preferences and pressures into their reading.

One could go further and suggest that Chaucer had meditated on the reader's activity along lines recently made fashionable by what is called 'reception theory'. As Eagleton summarises it (1983, p.76), this theory proposes that a text automatically

> involves us in a surprising amount of complex, largely unconscious labour: . . . we are all the time engaged in constructing hypotheses about the meaning of the text. The reader makes implicit connections, fills in gaps, draws inferences and tests out hunches; and to do this means drawing on a tacit knowledge of the world in general and of literary conventions in particular. The text itself is really no more than a series of 'cues' to the reader, invitations to construct a piece of language into meaning.

So phrased, the theory describes rather precisely the 'invitation' which Chaucer seems to issue knowingly in the *General Prologue,* where the degree of satirical sharpness that we interpret depends very much on how each of us works through the 'cues'. It would also tally with what has been said about the illusion of differing pilgrim voices in the *Tales:* as active readers we can take up the cues of small local touches of individualisation which are 'enough to make us supply differing styles' to the storytellers even though essentially 'the styles of all are a standard literary style' (Howard 1976, p.109).

I shall come back to some of these points later in this book. Meanwhile, it should begin to be apparent that, given Bloomfield's diagnosis of a fifteen-year period of jet-lag before new approaches affect study of Chaucer, the 'schools' of the most recent literary theory cannot be expected to provide a valid framework for the survey of critical debate that follows here in Part One. More predictably, familiar critical labelling is further hindered by the fact that medieval scholarship sometimes pursues controversies peculiar to itself. Thus one of the most combative areas of Chaucer study this century has centred on the claims of what are known as 'allegorical' critics. In due course we shall consider their distinctive approach, founded on biblical exposition in the Middle Ages. Another long-running dispute recently given fresh impetus has concerned the question, which of the early manuscripts of the *Tales* represents most accurately the state of the poem as Chaucer left it?

At first sight both biblical exposition and the priority of this or that manuscript might seem redundantly 'academic' matters. It is part of this book's function to explain why that is not altogether so (each issue, for instance, having relevance to the *Tales'* supposed 'debate on marriage'). At this stage, let us simply use the two issues to justify a division of Chaucer critics, by which I mean all who write professionally about his poetry, into schools. These two are like chalk and cheese. If I argue, with support from medieval theologians, that the Franklin's conception of a fine marriage in reality betrays his culpable worldly indifference to medieval religious orthodoxies on the subject, I am using one type of mental skill. By contrast: there is a link passage between the *Squire's Tale* and another tale where the next speaker (either Merchant or Franklin, depending on which manuscript we follow) comments on the Squire's 'gentillesse' and his own son's lack of it. If I deduce from the manuscripts that this passage was a late addition to the text and that it was probably written on a loose page, of uncertain authorship, I am using a different sort of mental skill.

Yet, specialists in these skills are not in total ignorance of each other. One specialist may play down the approach of another, but even an act of exclusion contributes implicitly to his own work. Eagleton (1983, p.31) startles us with the sweeping statement that 'English students in England today are "Leavisites" whether they know it or not', because 'that current' of criticism for which Leavis was a spokesman 'has entered the bloodstream of English studies'. To the extent that influential critical thinking gets into *every* critic's blood, therefore, a sorting-out into different critical schools can be patently naïve. But, just as Polonius in *Hamlet* strikes us as a buffoon when he talks of 'tragical-comical-historical-pastoral' drama, so it would tie us up in exasperating knots if I insisted that most modern Chaucer critics have been 'semi-historical, part-manuscriptical, subconsciously-new-critical' whether they know it or not.

In the present case there is not only the capaciousness of critics to reckon with: there is also the capaciousness of *The Canterbury Tales*. It seems only reasonable in this book to concentrate attention on the way critical positions most directly affect the more popular parts of the poem – always remembering, incidentally, that popularity-ratings tend to reflect the critical climate at a given time. Since considerable selectivity has been necessary, it may be helpful to attempt a telescopic review of approaches to the poem as a totality, before we begin.

In a common-sense judgement there is *no* totality. There is only an aborted plan: no return from Canterbury to Southwark, no free supper for the best story, and a dwindling-down from the projected four tales per pilgrim to just one each. If the poem's truncated state is emphasised, this leaves open two options for discussing it whole. The critic can assume the role of a post-mortem analyst and try to infer from conflicting manuscripts which, if any, of the fragmentary 'remains' might have been earmarked by Chaucer as potential return-journey items, or try to identify successive stages in the mortal collapse of the plan. Alternatively, one can risk the claim that the unfinishedness is somehow intentional, on the basis for example that the *outward* journey on a pilgrimage is paramount, with its quality of approach to a momentous spiritual destination. This would be more convincing if Chaucer's successor Lydgate had not seen fit to 'continue' the *Tales*, offering a first story for the return leg. But perhaps he missed the point?

Most critics have preferred to seek an overall principle expansive enough to override the fragmentary surviving state of the *Tales*. Since the stories are such a medley, it is least controversial to suppose they were conceived as a 'multiplicity': a generous literary act of creation in which it is over-optimistic to expect any cohesion other than an element of thematic concentration (e.g. on fortune, marriage or hypocrisy). The principle of 'multiplicity' attracts support from those who urge that *all* medieval Gothic art is composite in form, i.e. based on an accumulation of parts rather than focusing integrally upon a central point. *The Canterbury Tales* is certainly a composite in which differing views and genres are juxtaposed. But, because 'multiplicity' seems so unhelpfully vague, many scholars have looked for one particular juxtaposition pervading the *Tales* or even pervading Chaucer's whole output. Muscatine (1957) set the ball rolling by identifying an interplay between 'courtly' and 'bourgeois' styles in Chaucer. Phrases used in the titles of various books published since then show how fashionable it has been to place the *Tales* in the context of other polarities: *Art and Morals in Chaucer's Poetry; The Dialectic of 'Ernest' and 'Game'; The One and the Many in 'The Canterbury Tales'; Oppositions in Chaucer.*

It takes some nerve to assert, instead, any single governing principle. Actually, those ventured frequently turn out to be umbrellas covering multiplicity under another name. Thus 'Menippean Satire', an antique genre offered as one possible key, disconcertingly proves to mean ' literary hotch-potch'. Similarly if we speak of the *Tales* as a 'dramatic comedy', we only mean that the actor-pilgrims, with the poet somewhere in the background as a prompt, make 'speeches' within a 'plot' whose overall design remains open-ended. And, if pilgrimage itself, as an informing *concept* (rather than simply a mechanism for gathering storytellers together) is persuasive in relation to the beginning and end of the poem, it accounts less adequately for what passes between. Again, Howard's valiant bid to nail, in the words of his title, the 'idea' of *The Canterbury Tales* (1976) embraces too many subdivisions to allow a conclusive 'idea' to emerge, unless it be the model of a medieval labyrinth ('multiplicity' in a different guise once more?). Finally, there is a view that the *Tales* must be unified, in terms of doctrinal purpose. This view rules out genuine tensions or ambivalences on the grounds that no poet writing within the Christian culture of the Middle Ages would seriously present alternatives to single-minded love of God. Any contrary tendencies such as romantic passion must be interpreted as implicit deviations which help us to perceive true spiritual goals. This challenges the argument for ambiguous tension in the *Tales,* but seems still to leave us with a many-levelled hierarchy.

What, if anything, 'unifies' *The Canterbury Tales* therefore remains a taxing question. This book will not pursue it systematically. (In any case the question is not sacrosanct:

may just express a temporary brand of critical interest dominant within the twentieth century.) The questions treated here in Part One will be more limited. Isolating differing critical suppositions which have been brought to bear on Chaucer, we shall track debate through specific inquiries, such as the following. How does a 'psychological' reading of the Pardoner's contribution differ from readings by those who denounce the psychological approach? How do we discriminate between varying 'historical' critics who compete with each other (let alone with less-historical analysts) for the honour of explaining the meaning of the Wife of Bath? And what makes one critic assert that the *Nun's Priest's Tale* is an allegory of the fall of man, another that it is a witty satire on the human intellect?

In short Part One offers a practical survey intended to give the reader a sense of debate as it affects a number of tales, and thereby to equip that reader to take stock of his or her own critical assumptions and be wary of special pleading in other Chaucer commentary. 'Other commentary' includes the 'Appraisal' in Part Two of this book. If the reader detects weaknesses there after absorbing Part One, paradoxically the book will have succeeded in its purpose.

Source Study

'No other English medieval poet had such a complex pattern of indebtedness and independence in his relationship with major sources.' Few Chaucer critics would challenge Salter's axiom (1983, p.142), and awareness of source material is usually present even in the work of those who want us to study a tale essentially as a self-sufficient structure. It is broadly true that source study has 'changed direction' this century, 'from asserting the simple fact of Chaucer's reliance on earlier texts to speculating on the artistic implications of the way he uses them'; it is possibly also true that source study has 'slackened its pace'. However, in volume XV of the *Chaucer Review*, from which this opinion (Fleming 1980–1, p.287) is quoted, the pace of source-discussion can hardly be called indolent. Successive contributors seek to persuade us (a) that Chaucer's audience 'could be expected to know their Ovid and to hear it echoed in his work' (p.1); (b) that the Wife of *Bath* is calculated to invoke a traditional view of *baths* as places of sexual indulgence, exemplified in Ovid, Juvenal, St Jerome, and so on (pp.11–36); (c) that, when a red-hot implement scorches a student's backside in the *Miller's Tale,* we have a covert reference to a most dire contemporary medical treatment of anal disease – by cauterisation – expounded in a treatise 'so widely circulated . . . that Chaucer may well have known it' (p.228); and (d) that a 'famous passage' in the Book of Proverbs is a 'subtext' for the *Shipman's Tale* (pp.236, 244). Fleming himself is in quest of an untraced 'text' (condemning equestrian monks who rove beyond the cloister as fish out of water) which the *General Prologue* Monk scorns (pp.287–94).

The bedrock upon which all such propositions normally rest is explicit on page 236 of the same volume: Chaucer's 'originality often depends upon his precise manipulation of other texts *whose presence in his works,* if muted for twentieth-century readers, doubtless kindled the admiration of his first audience because they provided delightful *recognition of the familiar*'. I have italicised the more problematic phrases. A good deal of special pleading frequently accompanies claims concerning what other texts are actually present in Chaucer's narratives and how familiar they were. Precisely because misconceived source study can 'degenerate into an example of the indefatigable in pursuit of the untenable' (Schless 1974, p.184), we need to ask first whether Chaucer criticism has supplied groundrules by which to distinguish the tenable from the untenable.

This is no easy matter, even though everyone agrees that Chaucer is a conspicuously bookish poet. In one of his poems, he projects a comical image of himself consuming leisure hours, isolated from neighbours like a hermit, poring over books until his eyes are dazed [*House of Fame,* 647–60]. He often expresses a reverential attitude towards 'olde bookes' as reservoirs of knowledge. Also he sprinkles footnotes on background reading into his verse. For instance, introducing Pluto and Proserpina to oversee the climax of the *Merchant's Tale,* he declares, 'In Claudyan ye may the stories rede' of this duo [2232]: i.e. 'On Pluto, see further Claudian, *De Raptu Proserpinae,* 4th century'. The Man of Law pushily compares Chaucer (who is creating him!) with Ovid. Then, recollecting the competitive nature of the Canterbury storytelling game, he alludes cryptically to the legendary 'Pierides' who *lost* a song-contest against the Muses: 'Methamorphosios woot what I mene' [*Introduction to the Man of Law's Tale*, 93]: i.e. 'On the Pierides, see further Ovid, *Metamorphoses, V*, 294–678'.

Claudian and Ovid are among the authors mentioned in the personal library with which Chaucer credits himself. It includes some 'sixty bokes olde and newe' containing stories of virtuous women [*Prologue* to *The Legend of Good Women*, text G, 273ff.]. Taking the risk of responding too literally, I note that sixty large books fill only two five-foot bookshelves. Perhaps one should beware of over-estimating Chaucer's reading. Certainly he could neither have acquired nor have had access to anything like the massive collections of professional texts which a modern scholar takes for granted in studying him.

There is in fact growing concern that source studies should proceed more cautiously. Minnis is one critic who insists that sources remain central, because, if 'all the changes Chaucer made to his sources tend in a certain direction', then 'any interpretation which runs counter to that direction should be rejected' (1982, Preface). But Minnis equally and memorably insists that in the Middle Ages 'ideas did not travel in the air, in the water supply, or in the wine': every case of imputed 'influence' must be justified in terms of 'a specific process of transmission' (1981, pp.54, 62).

It is now recognised that knowledge of 'olde bookes' sometimes came to Chaucer in what we should call anthologies: handbooks of excerpts, or 'Selected Texts' from the past. Two such anthologies could account for Chaucer's readings in Claudian, and Seneca (Pratt 1947, 1966), and this in turn would make risky any hypothesis which assumed that he had read every word they wrote.

The case of Ovid brings up a related issue. It is fair to say that Chaucer 'owes more to Ovid than to any other classical author' (Fyler 1979, p.1), yet what triggers many an Ovid allusion is its appearance in an *intermediate* source, *The Romance of the Rose:* a text which along with Boethius's philosophical treatise Chaucer translated, and thereby absorbed radically into his literary bloodstream. And there is a further complication. Many medieval copies of Ovid's *Metamorphoses* were annotated with a formidable moralistic commentary. Should we therefore (like Hoffman 1966, and others) rigorously search for moral innuendo wherever Chaucer picks from that text? Or, if no such innuendo is provable, should we consider its absence a strong indication that Chaucer was temperamentally suspicious of attempts to attach moral exposition to classical – and perhaps to all – narrative (Cooper 1983, pp. 17–19)? The precise nature of his contact with Ovid thus becomes an important factor in assessing his conception of the poet's role.

We shall discuss that conception later. Meanwhile let us consider how critics have tackled the other problem: his immediate audience's 'recognition of the familiar'. The simple answer is, 'unconvincingly'; but only because the make-up of that audience and the realistic horizons of its reading-matter are so hard to determine. It is agreed that those who attended 'grammar' schools (a proportion of males only) learned Latin in anthologies containing texts such as *Aesop's Fables*. At higher levels of education, especially when we envisage the numerous trained 'clerkes' in London at this period as a leading element in Chaucer's public, the range of *possible* familiarity with learned texts yawns wide. That is to say, if a scorched backside in the *Miller's Tale* truly warrants cross-reference to a medical text in circulation around 1400, one cannot categorically deny that certain readers might have recognised the reference.

The probable extent of audience knowledge is partially explored by Coleman (1981), who properly stresses the variable nature of literacy at the time and voices the modern reader's desire 'to know what kind of philosophical problem an educated fourteenth-century public would recognize as familiar' (pp.22, 31). That question is I suppose especially pertinent to the *Nun's Priest's Tale* and the *Knight's Tale*. To answer it, Coleman goes first to inventories of books people owned. The evidence is better than nothing, yet we cannot be sure that the Duke of Gloucester actually *read* his 'six philosophy volumes' as against the 'nineteen romances' Coleman mentions in his instance (pp. 18–19). More persuasively, she considers what interests other poets attributed to that class of 'gentils' forming some portion of Chaucer's public. Langland was one contemporary who implied, with distaste, an 'opening up of theological issues to important men – who were not clerics, but who, none the less, discussed doctrinal matters at table'. Langland complained that they amateurishly questioned why God allowed evil to enter the world (pp.232–3). One might add that Chaucer's disciple Hoccleve wrote of an unseemly 'meddling' with points of doctrine among non-'gentil' people and *even among women* (in a propagandist poem, 'Address to Sir John Oldcastle', 137ff.). So the impression created in the tales themselves that literate or clerkish aspirations are percolating among lay people may not be just a fiction. We have a duke with intellectual views on Providence (*Knight's Tale*), a squire with ambitions in rhetoric (*Squire's Tale*), a 'gentil' woman who questions why God put sinister rocks in the world (Dorigen, *Franklin's Tale*), and a bourgeois woman who bandies scriptural quotation (the Wife of Bath). On the other hand it is significant that Langland says the doctrine-debating aristocrats also like 'blue' entertainers and listen to scurrilous stories (such as the *Miller's Tale?*); and further significant that Chaucer so often concedes the limits on his reader's appetite for learned discussion. Dorigen gives up her questions saying, 'To clerkes lete I al disputison' [*Franklin's Tale*, 890], while even the scholarly Nun's Priest refrains from pestering us with the thornier points in a discussion of free will.

All this seems to leave us with a medieval audience comprising (a) a socially various public, somewhat aware of the climate and language of learned thought but unlikely to savour anything too intellectual, and (b) a swathe of well-read clerks and cultured 'gentils', able to match Chaucer in at least segments of his own knowledge. Perhaps the Host in *The Canterbury Tales* epitomises and simultaneously caricatures the (a) public (Burnley 1983, pp.177, 181). He is conversant with learned language and ideas, but they are only skin-deep in him.

Part of the fun of reading the *Tales* is to rise to the challenge of allusive subtleties which the Host is too myopic to detect. Surrounding the comic re-run of Noah's Flood in the *Miller's Tale,* for example, are certain doctrinal nuances which seem to amount to 'a scholar's joke'; a joke which 'in its higher frequencies was probably heard only by scholars' ears' (Kolve 1984, p.198). Critics often lure us to the very highest frequencies of learned implication, to the very brink of sonar feasibility. They can easily persuade the modern reader to suppose Chaucer even more erudite – and thus more difficult – than he admittedly is. Fortunately source studies have been increasingly democratised. *The Romance of the Rose* is available in a translation by Charles Dahlberg. Students of the *Wife of Bath's*

Prologue and *Clerk's Tale* can consult sources in Miller (1977). And saucy continental tales to compare with Chaucer's fabliaux are now more accessible (Benson and Andersson 1971) than they were in Bryan and Dempster's *Sources and Analogues* (1941), which demanded knowledge of several foreign languages.

The tales were composed in an 'age of triumphant robberies in the practice of poetry' (Payne 1963, p.51). Comparison with sources which Chaucer definitely plundered can, of course, proceed without reference to what an audience would recognise, if the point is to clarify for ourselves what happens to the narrative 'loot' in the melting-pot of his imagination. From an initial pang of disappointment on discovering how faithfully he has imitated a source, we can go on to realise that this very fidelity actually highlights any deviations. They communicate his distinctive aims and qualities. There is only space here for me to sketch the critical problems in such analysis, by means of representative examples.

Let us see how a classic literary burglary, the *Knight's Tale*, provokes debate concerning the poet thief's intentions. Again the source text (Boccaccio's *Il Teseida*) can be checked in an English translation of the relevant portions (Havely 1980), to help establish whether 'even the smallest change is full of significance' (Salter 1983, p.145). One small early deviation may affect our whole view of Chaucer's Duke Theseus, who presides over the tale's events. When Theseus conquers a tyrant of Thebes, two youths named Palamon and Arcite of the defeated Theban dynasty come into his power. In Boccaccio, he first thinks of executing them to remove any possible future threat to his political safety. On second thoughts, he sentences them to life imprisonment but also gives instructions that they be *honourably treated, in reasonable comfort*. For Webb (1947), the fact that Chaucer both omits these instructions and inserts the Duke's refusal to contemplate ransoming his captives [1022–4], is a purposeful alteration to give Theseus a harsh 'hint of ignobility' beneath 'his veneer of nobility'.

This is precisely the sort of source crux from which divergent readings of the whole tale can stem. Following Webb's lead, we shall end up with a satirical romance centred on a high-handed Theseus whose chivalric prestige is undercut by suspected 'lapses' into tyranny. Alternatively we may minimise the note of harshness as a temporary thing qualified by the Duke's later acts of increasing benevolence (Fyler 1979, pp.142–3). Again, the harshness may be construed as incidental to Chaucer's larger intention, to present in the youths' wretched captivity an image of life itself as an imprisonment for humanity, from which the only release is a spiritual escape not available in the tale's pagan world (Kolve 1984, pp.98–102). Yet again, perhaps Theseus's increased severity is a legitimate extension of his duty to crush for good the disordered wickedness exemplified by Thebes; and, if the Duke's actions look arbitrary, that may underline the tale's interest in a Providence which is ultimately 'benevolent' in disturbingly inscrutable ways (Kean 1972, pp.8–9).

Consider another crux, a little further on in the story. Seeing the beautiful Emelye from their prison window, first Palamon and then Arcite conceives an instant passion for her. Within minutes their sworn brotherhood lies in ruins. Palamon rebukes Arcite for poaching 'his' lady-love: Arcite retorts with an 'olde clerkes' saying: "'who shal yeve a lovere any lawe?'" [1163–4]. Now, there is no such squabble at this stage in Boccaccio, since the two simply voice their yearnings for Emelye in parallel (Havely 1980, pp.113–14). Chaucer's substantial deviation here provokes two types of debate. One centres on whether he wants to differentiate the lovers by suggesting that Arcite is more opportunist, Palamon the 'worthier' idealist (see Frost, in Anderson, *Casebook*, pp.129–30). The other concerns the 'old saying' which Chaucer has slipped in here from his own translation of Boethius. If we go back to the *context* of the saying there, we find it used to explain why Orpheus, trying to rescue his beloved Eurydice from the underworld, could not keep his 'covenant' not to look at her during their upward journey. Moreover, Orpheus's failure, says Boethius's treatise, signifies that humans must set their sights on the clear light of spiritual goals and not drop their minds towards 'erthly thinges' which lead down to hell (Lumiansky 1955, pp.42–3).

Chaucer has superimposed a piece of Boethius on Boccaccio. The question is, are we to connect Arcite with Orpheus as one who misdirects himself towards earthly passions? There are certainly occasions in the *Tales* where Chaucer dislodges and imports one brick from a source *without* reference to the whole wall surrounding it. But so many bricks (like the present specimen) from Boethius accumulate in the *Knight's Tale* that the poem's total relationship with that philosophical edifice can be infinitely debated – probably most consummately, to date, by Salter (1983).

The pilgrim-poet's remarks when introducing his 'own' *Tale of Melibee* may be worth a mention here. He is about to offer a version of a rather popular edifying story, which he declares has been presented 'in sondry wyse' by different writers – just as the gospel accounts of Christ's life vary slightly. He professes to be terribly anxious lest members of his audience should notice that he may draft in the odd extra proverb and may not use exactly 'the same wordes' as they have 'herd' elsewhere. This passage [*Sir Thopas*, 940–66] has a faintly ludicrous edge. The Host has just described the pilgrim–poet's first storytelling attempt as sub-literary rubbish. Chaucer's retaliation is a mock-deferential joke expressing the unlikely notion that he faces an audience of expert literary examiners ready to subtract marks for the slightest 'mis-quotation' of his source. Perhaps there is only a local, pointed irony – that in *this* tale (as opposed to any other) we shall indeed find him exercising no subtle reshaping of received narrative. But it is tempting to wonder whether he winks mischievously at anyone who would presume to unravel the wizardry of his source-juggling, from 1400 till kingdom come.

Where he *does* signal a specific source, however subsidiary, the implications for criticism can nevertheless be quite important. A good instance is the advice in the *Wife of Bath's Tale:* 'Redeth Ovyde', to discover the 'remenant' of the story of Midas.

The Wife is reviewing a multitude of claims about what it is that women most desire. One idea is that women want to be considered discreet, able to keep secrets. But, according to the Wife of Bath, all female claims to confidentiality are blown to bits by the story of Midas, whose wife alone knew of the ass's ears which disfigured him: bursting with the secret, she had to rush out to tell it to a pool of water [950–82].

In Ovid it is Midas's barber, not Mrs Midas, who discloses the secret, to a hole in the ground whence reeds grow up and spread the news by their 'whispering'. The Wife of Bath has misremembered or deliberately changed the story. In the light of the details in the *Metamorphoses*, we may want to argue that it is characteristic of her that she should 'misquote a story from Ovid in an attempt to prove her point' (Slade, in Anderson, *Casebook,* p.166). We can go further if we infer that 'the remenant' of Midas's legend – the wall from which Chaucer has borrowed some bricks – is substantially relevant.

For one thing, Midas, like the Wife, was addicted to revelry. Next, we note that, when Bacchus offered him the right to choose any gift, he asked that all he touched should turn to gold – a mercenary streak the Wife may be said to share. Later, Ovid's Midas was punished with his ass's ears for stupidly judging the music of Pan (rustic deity of fertility) superior to that of Apollo (god of music and poetry). Midas's dud 'ear' for music relates wittily to the Wife's own deafness, while his repeated failure to make prudent *choices* both links with a moment of choice occurring at the climax of the Wife's tale, and insinuates how she herself has chosen an 'imperfect' lifestyle (Hoffman 1966, pp.145–9). A source that looked merely incidental yields a cross-light that plays over the Wife of Bath's entire performance.

To round off this section let us ask, what are the poet's major distinguishing features to which source study leads the critics? Compared with Boccaccio, they have found Chaucer less sentimental and more objective, the *Knight's Tale* presenting 'the quality and causes of human suffering' and 'dilemmas of pain and belief' more profoundly than the *Teseida* (Salter 1983, p.149). (A recent editor of *Troilus*, B.A. Windeatt, also finds Chaucer expressing a greater 'vehemence' than Boccaccio, especially in projecting 'the textures of any emotional scene'.) In comparison with Dante, whom he also sometimes raided, Chaucer is found to emphasise 'people and not doctrines', the world of affairs rather than the overarching doctrinal vision which subsumes that world in the *Divine Comedy* (Schless 1974, pp.219–20; Howard 1976, pp. 41–5).

To the objection that if such qualities are in the *Tales* we need no source critics to demonstrate them, it may be answered that source study is only one species of that process of literary comparison which goes on in our heads all the time. In any case, source study of Chaucer is unlikely to cease, for two reasons. First, its character is open to modification by new waves of critical taste. Modern Structuralist criticism, for instance, introduces fresh considerations. Structuralists look for 'the underlying rule-systems of a literary text', the 'central meaning' informing every aspect of the work, its 'deep structure' (Eagleton 1983, pp.109, 112). The *Nun's Priest's Tale* and its sources have been analysed in these terms by Brewer. He perceives in the traditional fable of the cock and the fox a 'deep structure of reversal' in which, archetypally, 'Strong *a* fools weak *b*: but then *b* fools *a*'. This pattern of *reversal* is an 'inner point' to which we can refer most of Chaucer's elaborations, such as the cock's failure to act upon his own conviction that his dream of a fox-like adversary must be prophetic (1979 pp.90–106).

The second, fundamental reason why source study will continue is the absorbing, tantalising elusiveness of that complex pattern of indebtedness to other writings which the tales everywhere display.

Retrieving literary conventions

It is a salutary jest that diehard medievalists 'often think if a medieval work appeals to a modern taste the appeal must be mistaken, and so scurry off to find an antiquated taste for it to appeal to' (Howard 1976, p.369). In truth we are more often urged to make allowances for now defunct 'conventions' in Chaucer's poetry which do *not* appeal to modern taste. This applies, for example, to various compositional features which he owes to the handbooks on rhetoric – in effect the 'literary theory' of his day.

Since rhetoric sounds like a synthetic additive, which we know is widely used in literature but which we would rather not think about, there is a real need for wholesome critical guidance on its significance in Chaucer. Payne's discussion is helpful (1963). He explains the rhetoricians' emphasis on techniques of stylistic elaboration and analyses Chaucer's somewhat equivocal attitude to the basic premises of medieval literary rhetoric, i.e. the supposition that poetry constitutes an orderly presentation and emotive embellishment of morally pointed narrative or of known truths. Knight (1973) is an example of a critic who conducts a close reading of some of the tales in a way that respects the poet's intimate skill in manipulating devices of eloquence. Not infrequently Chaucer plays such arch games with them that they become crucial in interpretative debate. Thus, the Franklin's elaborate apology for his 'rude speche' in his prologue [716–26] contains so much clever rhetoric as to display 'an ostentation in his modesty' which according to Spearing prevents him from being the truly *gentil* person he aspires to be (1966, pp.16–19). And this in turn contributes to an argument that the ensuing tale is full of ironies at the expense of the Franklin.

However, rhetoric is not a pass-key to the artistry of the *Tales* generally, perhaps because for Chaucer rhetorical precepts became 'problems in the practice of poetry more than they were rules for the conduct of it' (Payne 1963, p.89). Some of the 'problems' seem to be on view in the *Squire's Tale,* whose speaker is hypersensitive about the 'art of speche' [104] and is dangerously prone to rhetorical expatiation. He even takes eight lines to remind himself that a storyteller must avoid 'prolixitee' in order to reach the nub or 'knotte' of a tale before interest wanes [401–8].

Now, Chaucer is everywhere self-conscious about narrative *pace.* Moreover the Squire's knot-metaphor, itself borrowed probably from Horace's *Art of Poetry,* is instructive in two ways: it suggests the importance Chaucer attributed to narrative *dénouement* (a word which actually means 'un-knotting'), and it reminds us of the multiple *strands* which interact in a well-woven climax. In fact skilled knot-work has been thought a major feature in some of the best of Chaucer's shorter tales, such as the Pardoner's. They culminate at great speed and yet with a seeming inevitability made possible by the way various strands have been carefully exposed to us beforehand (Bishop, in Anderson, *Casebook,* pp.215–16). Yet such skills were scarcely derivable from the rhetorical handbooks. These have little to say about techniques of crescendo, apart from what is implicit in such general advice as 'Let the mind's inner compass circumscribe the whole area of the subject matter in advance' (Geoffrey of Vinsauf, in Murphy 1971, p.34).

If critics have found Chaucer ambivalent in relation to rhetorical conventions of embellishment, the same is true of his relation to the function of narrative as 'exemplification': i.e. the medieval convention by which 'a story . . . is pre-eminently an example which illustrates some truth or concept concerning human life and conduct'. I am quoting Burrow, who argues that the tales complicate and subvert this exemplifying-function. He suggests that the narrow-minded, personal responses of the Host and other pilgrims to successive stories make us suspect that what *anyone* thinks a tale exemplifies is skewed by 'his own circumstances and preoccupations'. Equally, the storytellers themselves are seen to bring private purposes into their tales (lambasting other pilgrims; advocating female sovereignty; and so on) which undermine the idea that a tale can be objectively exemplary (1971 pp. 78–92).

In the same vein, Pearsall notes that the genres represented in the *Tales* (e.g. fable, fabliau, saint's legend, romance) had traditionally served 'some truth already known to be true, whether it be of an elevating or degrading kind'. He considers that Chaucer attempted to 'release narrative from this external pressure, and to allow it a significance of its own' (1970, p.177). He adds, however, that 'not all the Tales attempt to do this'. Here lurks a major critical problem. For although it is clear that, say, the Nun's Priest's and Pardoner's performances in different ways scramble the reader's responses to moral signification, it is much less clear whether the Franklin's narrative illustration of *gentillesse* is also somehow sabotaged by Chaucer. Some critics even find ironies complicating the ostensibly firm moral significance of a tale such as the Man of Law's (concerning a Christian heroine's formidable endurance). But this would be one of Pearsall's exceptions – a tale which unambiguously proclaims 'a profound orthodoxy of belief' and which demands our full acquiescence in its symphony of rhetoric (p.178).

Sympathetic inquiry furnishes us with knowledge of the conventions I have been discussing, if not with easy conclusions about Chaucer's ways with them. However, the *stylistic* conventions he worked with are notably difficult to pinpoint at this distance. Burnley asks what 'levels of style' are inherent in Chaucer (1983, pp.177–200), and distinguishes broadly two. One is *heigh stile* or *faire speche*, appropriate to *curteis* discourse characterised by eloquent sentence structure and graciousness of diction (which includes a surprising degree of familiarity with technical *termes* of rhetoric, philosophy, and so on). The other is *rude, bare* or *pleyn* style associated with *boystous* or *lewed* (uneducated) discourse. Individual tales do not, of course, fall pat into one or other style, because the overall 'authorial voice' in the poetry is persuasively 'decorous', inclining generally to *faire speche*. Yet at any given moment, as when the Host shows exceeding deference in asking the Prioress for her tale, a passage may significantly evoke either level.

Some of these findings complement the view of stylistic convention set forth in Muscatine's vintage study, *Chaucer and the French Tradition* (1957). But, whereas Burnley gives us a sense of how Chaucer's styles may reflect actual perceptions of language as a marker of social status or social ideals among his contemporaries, Muscatine was more concerned to stress the literary inheritance underlying even the most lifelike features of style in such tales as the Reeve's (pp.197–8).

Muscatine wanted to squash an earlier idea that Chaucer's poetic career was a glorious escape from the shackles of artifice into the fresh air of 'realism' which the tales were thought to represent. He claimed instead that Chaucer drew throughout on two major stylistic conventions in French literature: (1) the courtly tradition of romance, typified by high idealism, formal presentation of love and other emotions, non-representational flavour, and static rhetorical elegance of description; and (2) the 'bourgeois' tradition of racy short fiction, typified by prosaic attention to tangible physical detail, turbulent cartoon-like action, irreverent tone, and a cast of predictable tradesmen, priests, peasants and wenches. Muscatine found the *Knight's Tale* an elaborate version of (1), while the *Reeve's Tale*, *Canon's Yeoman's Tale* and *Wife of Bath's Prologue*, raised (2) to a new level of art. Other tales (e.g. the *Merchant's Tale* and *Nun's Priest's Tale*) modulated between (1) *and* (2) in a complex and challenging 'mixed style'.

Thanks to the compact brilliance of Muscatine's commentary, his insistence on the importance of literary traditions has continued to reverberate through Chaucer criticism. One focus for debate about their importance is the question of characterisation. Above all, the *General Prologue* has been a critical arena, strewn with casualties especially amongst those who have supposed the pilgrim portraits a 'modern' triumph of wholesale naturalistic creation.

The naturalistic fallacy (as some would think it) goes back at least to Dryden, who in 1700 felt the pilgrims so lifelike that he might have 'supp'd with them at the Tabard' (Anderson, *Casebook*, p.21). Subsequently the stereotypes within Chaucer's characters grew more visible, but Kittredge spoke influentially of the poet's genius for 'endowing each of them with an individuality that goes much beyond the typical' (1915, p.154). A 1948 commentary on the *Prologue* tots up the balance as though each pilgrim had a double Janus-face, half looking back to conventional type and half looking forward to naturalism. Thus the Friar is 'individual' because of his merry songs, lisp, and twinkling eyes; and a satirical 'type' in his greed and professional hypocrisy: but all in all still 'so real that we can think of him only as . . . a distinct and living person' (Bowden 1948, p.141).

However, Mann's 1973 analysis makes this critical terminology sound woolly and inaccurate. She identifies 'Estates Satire' (i.e. writings which expressed the failings attributed to particular professions) as a primary convention in the *Prologue*. In her view, the fact that Friar Huberd cultivated a lisp 'To make his Englissh sweete upon his tonge' [265] derives from the satirists' customary insinuation that friars went in for too much sweet-talking flattery (pp.37–41). Even Huberd's convivial musicianship, which is *not* in the satiric stereotype, she considers parodic of the friars' profession, since their founder called them 'God's minstrels'. So, 'literary analysis, rather than an appeal to real life' strikes her as essential to the interpretation of such details (p.45).

In denying the notion that Chaucer abolished conventional procedures of characterisation at one swoop, Mann is not denying his creativity. She explains how he uniquely blurs the normally destructive impetus of the satirical formulae he is adapting, for example by expressing the pilgrims' professional failings as though they were forms of 'expertise' to be proud of. We are lured towards admiration because the damaging *impact* of their expertise on society is played down, and because we are often confined within their own public estimate of themselves. The *Prologue* constructs pilgrim 'façades' without supplying the satirist's explicit ammunition to penetrate them.

Mann also explores Chaucer's creative response to standard recommendations about character description in books on rhetoric. Budding writers were instructed there in the art of describing either 'for praise' or 'for censure' (*ad laudem vel ad vituperium)*. You were adv sed to eulogise a character's beauty/virtue, *or* to deno nce a person's ugliness/moral turpitude. Not altogether w thout poetic precedent, Chaucer saw the advantage of doing b >th at once. Hence, by presenting 'morally reprehensible traits in terms of enthusiastic appreciation', he could confuse admiration with censure 'in such a way as to reproduce the complex response which we normally have to real people' (p.184).

One might add to this absorbing argument the footnote that one rhetorician (Geoffrey of Vinsauf, mentioned in the *Nun's Priest's Tale)* actually takes us very close to the strategy Mann outlines. 'If you wish to inveigh fully against foolish people', he suggests, 'attack in this way: praise, but facetiously; accuse, but bear yourself good humouredly'. If you want to mock an ignoramus who pretends to be an intellectual, do so *covertly:* 'anticipating his desire, greet him as "master"; nonetheless, in the meantime, laugh at him obliquely. Peck at him, as it were, with the "beak" of your hands . . .' (in Murphy 1971, pp. 49–50).

Oblique 'pecking' laughter is surely a hallmark of Chaucer's poetry in the *Prologue* and beyond. We have returned to the rhetorical background, which is possibly too prominent in this section. After all, critics detect hosts of literary conventions in the *Tales,* including narrative methods inherited from the English verse romances, the whole phenomenon of courtly love, and the legacy of anti-feminist writings. Some can be discussed in later sections, but the reader should note that just one word can lead into the storehouse of convention, as Pearcy (1973–4) shows when he analyses the expectations generated by Chaucer's description of the Franklin as a 'vavasour'.

In any case, the debate about the conventionality or otherwise of Chaucer's characterisation takes priority because it helps us both to refine our attitudes towards 'realism' in literature, and to perceive possibilities that enrich our reading. Admittedly, anyone with a glossary can enjoy the vibrant description of Alisoun, coffee-bar heroine of the *Miller's Tale.* We are trained to relish the thought that her face shines like a new-minted coin [3255–6]: a lovely pristine sparkle – only, what's the *price* of her virtue, and aren't new coins ready for *circulation?* But, according to the scholar of medieval convention, we shall miss a whole layer of art if we do not see how her monetary gleam wittily modifies the customary golden radiance of a medieval romantic heroine, and indeed how her entire description plays off against standard formulae of female beauty (Brewer 1955).

As Minnis puts it, the plain fact is that Chaucer's 'extensive "defamiliarization" (notably of literary convention and of genre) cannot be appreciated until we know what was "familiar" to him' (1981 p.54).

Medieval intellectual contexts

In the preceding section we mentioned the musical abilities of the *Prologue* Friar, who sings and harps with a cheerful twinkle in his eyes [266–7]. For one kind of Chaucer critic, Huberd the tavern-haunting harpist links ironically with the biblical David, known to medieval thought as God's harpist and singer of the Psalms (Huppé 1964, p.37).

The basis for avowing such a connection would be that the primary context for medieval poetry is religious culture, especially the Bible and its 'exegesis' or exposition by the early Christian 'Fathers' (*Patres*). Criticism grounded in that exposition is thus 'exegetical' or 'Patristic'. It is otherwise 'historical', in that it concentrates on doctrines disseminated throughout the medieval period; or, alternatively, 'allegorical', in that it claims the period's literature characteristically *veils* a core of moral truth beneath the skein or shell of pleasurable fiction. Since the 'veil' idea derives from St Augustine, the approach is 'Augustinian', though still another epithet amongst this bewildering heap is 'Robertsonian' – after the American critic Robertson, who consolidated it all in his monumental *Preface to Chaucer* (1962).

In what directions does an 'allegorical' reading of the *Tales* take us? For a start, it gives prominence to some remarks at the end of the teasing fable of Chauntecleer the cockerel. There the Nun's Priest advises any who would consider his fable 'a folye', to grasp 'the moralite' – the 'fruyt' as opposed to the 'chaf' – remembering St Paul's dictum that 'al that writen is, / To oure doctrine it is ywrite, ywis' [3438-43].

Allegorical critics set out to discover the fruits of doctrine cunningly lodged within Chaucer's chaff. In the case of the *Nun's Priest's Tale*, this means we should reflect seriously, for example, on a passage of humorous reproach to Venus for apparently abandoning Chauntecleer to the clutches of a fox despite his erotic labours in her cause, performed 'Moore for delit than world to multiplye' [3342–6]. That is, Chauntecleer put sex (with his seven wives, especially Pertelote) before procreation. In so doing he flouted a central tenet of marriage doctrine as expounded in the *Parson's Tale*. There we read that marriage was instituted 'to multiplye mankynde to the service of God' [882]. Even marital sex specifically for the purpose of procreation is tinged with 'venial synne' because of its concomitant 'delit', but a married couple going to bed '*oonly* for amorous love' or torrid 'delit', wallow into '*deedly* synne' [941–2]. And a man who has greater love for his wife than for God is an idolater [859].

Whether or not we are amazed by the clarity of mental intent which this 'official' theology demands within the sex-act in a pre-contraception era, it is clear that Chauntecleer stands guilty, if we press charges of 'delit' extracted from the Parson. And, for allegorical critics, the *Parson's Tale* is a compendium of Chaucer's ulterior orthodoxies, a warehouse of those moral 'fruits' which elsewhere in the *Tales* he packages in the glossy wrappings of fiction. However, the Parson's privileged status has been disputed. One may object, for instance, that the tales modify each other to yield a succession of 'tensions and contradictions' which 'relativise our values until we reach the absolute values of the Parson . . . but in assigning these absolute values to a character *within* the *Tales* . . . Chaucer in one sense makes these values relative too' (Mann 1973, p.190).

The allegorical school would protest that the Parson's voice *is* authoritative because he crowns and transcends the tales by stating the moral guidelines for humankind's spiritual pilgrimage, so as to 'knytte up al this feeste' of storytelling 'and make an ende' [*Parson's Prologue*, 31–47]: and we have already seen the significance of the 'knot' in Chaucer's narrative method. Secondly, tensions or contradictions or relative values would be thought alien to medieval literature, which was deeply ingrained with a pattern of thought whereby the world is a ladder designed to lead us systematically up to God (Robertson 1962, pp.6ff.).

Let us return to the *Nun's Priest's Tale*. Chauntecleer is, allegorically, not just a guilty sensualist: he is a second Adam, an errant Christian who repeats the Fall by subduing his reason to the beauty of Pertelote (so bewitchingly 'scarlet reed' around the eyes is she [3161]). Thus weakened, he is trapped by the enticements of the Devil (the fox), but retrieves salvation by recovering his reason (his wits). Allusions to the creation of man [3187–8] and to Eve's responsibility for original sin [3257–8] are taken to reinforce the tale's moral 'fruit' – a lesson on 'the confusion of God's order by surrender to the pleasure principle' (Huppé 1964, pp.174ff.).

To a non-allegorical critic, the weightiness of this reading is really more of a 'deadweight'. For it relegates to the status of 'chaff' the poem's distinctive mass of playful rhetorical elaboration. Perhaps we should therefore entertain instead the paradox that the 'fruit' of the tale *is* its 'chaff' (Donaldson 1960, pp.147–50).

Before discussing the implications of this critical stalemate, let us glance at another allegorical reading, which demonstrates the method's reliance on theological analysis. This example concerns the Wife 'of biside Bathe', who has had five husbands and who in her prologue mentions an encounter beside a well between Jesus and a five-times-married Samaritan woman [14–23 (see John 4:3–26)]. Jesus offered the woman spiritual 'living water', which at first baffled her literal imagination. When she then asked for such water, Jesus told her to call her husband. On her answering that she had none, he commented that indeed, since she had had five husbands, 'he whom thou now hast is not thy husband'. It is not perfectly clear to us whether she is cohabiting with a sixth partner. It is not clear to the Wife of Bath what Jesus 'mente' either, but her assumption that the man referred to was the fifth husband makes her anxious to discover the maximum permissible quota of remarriages.

Now, Robertson finds the Wife of Bath a 'deaf' literalist (like the Samaritan woman was initially). What she is deaf to is the import of the passage in scriptural commentary. There, the woman represents unconverted humanity; the well is worldly pleasure; and the instruction to 'call her husband' means she should summon up her neglected reason, though the five husbands may also symbolise her previous indulgence in the five senses (1962, pp. 320–21). Unable to hear what the Bible 'mente', the Wife of Bath emerges as a 'hopelessly carnal' literalist who allows body and will to dominate over spirit and reason.

This exposition gains credibility from the fact that the pilgrims acknowledge how the Wife has broached 'scole-matere' of 'greet difficultee' [*Friar's Prologue*, 1271–2]. But it will also be apparent that, under this ultra-exegetic light, the Wife of Bath like Chauntecleer is in danger of melting down to a mere blob of anti-sensual morality. Under this same light, Palamon and Arcite in the *Knight's Tale* disclose not the pathos of emotional suffering in love, but a sinful abandonment of reason as they give in to idolatrous passion. Moreover, in the *Franklin's Tale*, the 'humble, wys accord' whereby Arveragus wishes to preserve an amorous deference to his wife Dorigen [791–8] actually betrays the Franklin's immoral sentimentality because it negates the 'hierarchy of marriage' integral to Chaucer's society and established in canon law and theology (Robertson 1974). Again, doctrinal thought can be used to prove that Dorigen has no obligation to stand by her compromising vow to make love to squire Aurelius if he removes the coastal rocks which so frighten her (Gaylord 1964).

The validity of such approaches is an important matter if, as Burrow says, in our ignorance of Latin theology we are not to be haunted by a suspicion that we are 'debarred from some deep and important "level" of meaning accessible only to trained medievalists' (1971, pp.78–9). Burrow goes on to argue that Chaucer distinctly prefers a literal to an allegorical mode of expression. Many critics think that Chaucer was sceptical about the moral allegorisation of narrative. They find it instructive that when he approaches the frontiers of allegory, as in the case of the Old Man in the *Pardoner's Tale*, he is reluctant actually to cross. Or they note how a problematic allegorical dimension in the *Clerk's Tale* implies that allegory demands 'a stronger didacticism than Chaucer's urbanity ever makes possible to him' (Kean 1972, p.129). More generally, it is suspected that Robertsonians prejudice their reading by presupposing, before they experience the poetry, that it will yield a particular kind of (doctrinal) coherence (Rogers 1980).

On the other hand, the allegorical school has certainly created a climate which heightens our concentration on what

Chaucer is up to when he plays doctrinal and scriptural nuances provocatively into the *Tales*. In that climate, even a non-allegorical critic is more likely to winkle out nuggets of biblical wit, as does Brewer in commenting on the Nun's Priest's description of Chauntecleer's seven hens as the cockerel's 'sustres and his paramours' [2867]. This mischievously (rather than solemnly, as an earlier critic thought) recalls a phrase from the Song of Songs (4:9–12) in which a sensuous lover cries, 'Thou hast ravished my heart, *my sister, my spouse*.' Medieval theologians found ways of allegorising this scriptural love-song into respectability, but Brewer points us to the literal joke that Chauntecleer's hens are (as happens in hen-runs) actually both his sisters and his spouses – 'a forbidden incestuous relationship apparently recommended by sacred Scripture' (1979, pp.102–3).

In this perspective, doctrinal nuance constitutes not a *fruit* which is the essence of a tale, but a *fruity flavour* enriching a tale's bouquet. By the same token, we should find fruitiness rather than a sharp moral tang when a lusty student in the Miller's Tale invites an incongruous comparison with the angel Gabriel by singing the Annunciation song. Overall, the doctrinal influence on the *Tales* would 'consist in providing occasional symbols which by their rich tradition enhance the poetic contexts they appear in' (Donaldson 1960, pp. 134–5).

However, a major new direction pertinent to all this has been developed by Kolve (1984). He suggests that the tales purposefully enclose traditional symbolic visual images within stories that are not themselves primarily symbolic. These implicit visual images involve a medieval sign-language ranging from the popular to the learned. They coincide with a tale's major surface-narrative images and thus enhance what is central in our imaginative *memory* of each story. Thus in the *Knight's Tale* one major narrative image is that of 'imprisonment'. The poem draws together two traditional images: (1) passionate love as something which enfetters lovers in the bonds of desire (specifically Palamon and Arcite, who are also literally political captives); and (2) life itself or the mortal body as a 'foule prisoun' [3061] which – as Marvell was to put it – manacles the soul. By contrast, in the *Miller's Tale* Chaucer forestalls the potential emblematic force of animal and other imagery as if by an 'act of imaginative exclusion' (p.216). That exclusion of the imagery's moral possibilities is part of this tale's point. It is an example of a text whose artistic mode, for Kolve, does *not* supply the kind of context which supports a moral-symbolic reading. So, too, he considers the Nun's Priest's postscript about 'fruyt' and 'doctrine' 'outrageously too grand' for its context and 'meant to amuse, rather than to send us scurrying to the tomes of the Fathers' (pp. 76–8).

Finally, let us briefly review a few other areas of debate germane to this section. Prior to Kolve's ideas about visual traditions came an argument, based on the study of form and structure in Gothic architecture, that Chaucer's poetry never displays organic consistency. It is instead full of independent segments which jostle together (as Pluto and Proserpina rub shoulders with a Lombard knight and his wife in the *Merchant's Tale*) in defiance of any modern taste for integrated illusion (Jordan 1967).

Chaucer's relationship with Gothic art remains a fertile area of discussion. So does his relationship with pagan thought. Chaucer's whole view of pagan antiquity is set in its historical context by Minnis (1982). His book also discusses astrology, a topic anxiously pondered by medieval churchmen and of somewhat ambivalent status in the *Tales*. Since the Franklin makes hostile remarks about supposed astral influence over the world, and since Chaucer throws a sudden left hook at 'pagan' horoscopic astrology in his own Astrolabe treatise, are we to be critical of the Wife of Bath's claim that she inevitably followed the lifestyle the stars inclined her toward (Wood 1979, p.205; Bronson 1960, pp. 12–16)?

Of all the scientific contexts first assembled for Chaucer by Curry, probably astrology has grown the most problematic. But he discussed so well the presence of medieval medicine and physiognomy (i.e. the character-implications of bodily attributes) in the *Tales* that critics mesmerised, for instance, by the *General Prologue's* insinuation of sexual impotence in the Pardoner unfailingly refer somewhere along the line to Curry's enticing chapter 'The Pardoner's Secret' (1926, pp. 54–70).

Social and political historicism

Given the blank disinterest usually provoked by topical allusion in writers such as Alexander Pope, readers may be relieved to hear that Chaucer's poetry is widely agreed to be 'bare of direct allusions to specific contemporary people and events' (Muscatine 1972, p. 26). However, scholars abhor a vacuum, so there have been diverse attempts to slot the *Tales* back into Chaucer's biographical, social and political circumstances.

One strategy was to comb history for events and notorious scandals which could be made to fit the narratives, and, behold, here was 'topical allegory'. By this method, Chauntecleer's adversary in the *Nun's Priest's Tale* was a *colfox* in honour of the treacherous Nicholas Colfox, implicated in the assassination of the Duke of Gloucester at Calais (Hotson 1924). That belongs to a once-thriving chapter of scholarship that is now largely closed, though variations of it still occasionally surface.

Critics of that persuasion have usually claimed that topical skeletons are expediently hidden in the cupboards of Chaucer's poems because he is too prudent to risk making them obvious. Nowadays his prudence is more often felt to be the mark of a poet ideologically wary or detached by temperament, sensibly refraining altogether from reference to gunpowdery issues. This would help explain how he kept his head (in both senses) through a potentially delicate public career by contrast with, for example, Richard Lyons – a comparable figure who was an influential wine-merchant but who got embroiled in the smouldering politics of the time and was murdered in 1381 (Du Boulay 1974, p. 42).

Chaucer does sometimes touch upon controversial matters, as when he expresses distaste for an undignified scramble for lucrative priestly appointments that was going on in London [*General Prologue*, 507–14]. But this, like his hostility to friars, does not significantly distinguish his voice from the general run of satirical anti-clericalism which was countenanced in his culture. Similarly, although he was acquainted with known Lollards (i.e. a group eventually stamped out because of its 'evangelical' ideas about reform of the Church), that alignment does not emerge as a propagandist strain in his poetry (Du Boulay, pp. 44–7).

Along with topical allusion, there is another water-under-the-bridge school of historical criticism. It centres on the work of Manly, who used Chaucer's own biography to hunt down real-life models for the pilgrims (1926). Manly is nowadays extravagantly derided for this on the grounds that Chaucer was not, and by the canons of literary convention could never have been, a poet of simple photographic observation. Another objection is that we learn nothing analytically useful from conjectures such as (a) that Chaucer's Sergeant of the Law equals an astute land-dealing lawyer Sir Thomas Pynchbek whose Lincolnshire property was near that of Chaucer's sister-in-law, or (b) that the Sergeant's companion the Franklin equals a certain John Bussy, who paralleled the Franklin in holding public offices and was Pynchbek's associate. Yet perhaps we should not under-estimate the benefits of such work, in terms of better understanding, for example, what it meant in the 1380s to be, as were Bussy and the Franklin, a 'sheriff' (a medieval official both like and unlike his frequently 'bent' gun-toting television counterpart).

As it happens, Chaucer probably acquired some degree of legal training. On that basis one can build a fragile supposition that there is something of himself in the legal-minded Franklin. One can meditate a possible tense connection between the *Franklin's Tale*'s climactic event, where Aurelius releases Dorigen from her quasi-legal contract to commit adultery with him, and a murky episode in Chaucer's recorded life whereby the poet was released from an accusation of 'rape' by Cecelia Chaumpaigne (Blenner-Hassett 1953).

Unverifiable speculation is the Achilles' heel of this kind of biographical criticism. At a broader level it is just possible that the 'courtly clichés' and the 'posturing' which weigh down the *Squire's Tale* betray a poet out of key with the aristocracy – give us 'a glimpse of the "bourgeois" Chaucer, the "new man" of the fourteenth century' (Howard 1976, p.267). We can flirt with a hypothesis that the poet's social advancement into court acceptance (though by no means unique) left him subconsciously insecure, and prompted 'his notable ambivalence towards his own culture' because he was dislodged from a firm root in the theoretical categories of medieval society (Brewer 1968, pp. 70–1). Yet the same critic notes Chaucer's strong affiliations with the 'gentil' sector of society; and another affirms that his mercantile origins in the wine-trade would not have diminished his acquired status as 'gentilhomme' (Du Boulay, pp. 36–7).

These questions of social orientation, as we shall see, are up for radical revision. For the moment, we shall glance at other perennial species of historicism.

One species concerns the orality of Chaucer's poetry. We are aware as we read that the tales combine literary bookishness with what Howard calls 'voiceness' (1976, p.66) in the sense that we 'hear' stories told aloud by different speakers. Chaucer seems paradoxically to attend to a listening audience's response in the very act of writing. Historically this connects with the fact that live recitation of poetry was a widespread social phenomenon. Today's highbrow live poetry-reading gets us nowhere near it. No doubt Chaucer developed a talent for oral expression as an Esquire in the royal household (*c*. 1368), because such squires were looked to for varieties of court entertainment. No one can say whether the tales themselves were read aloud at court. But the 1930s discovery of his poetry's oral dimension has since focused attention on how the verse is textured for easy 'listenability', how Chaucer creates an engagingly sociable communication which hooks us as cleverly as a gifted after-dinner speaker (Spearing 1972, pp. 16–27; Bronson 1960, pp. 29–32, 66–7). Once acquainted with the language we shall find that his quasi-oral poetry is, like a congenial computer, 'user-friendly'. The oral background also emphasises a conundrum in our response to the *Tales:* that is, the ambiguity about just whose voice, at any given moment, we believe we hear.

Another evergreen historical approach consists, simply, in the collection and interpretation of data which are integral to Chaucer's language. One could call it an 'archaeological' activity (literally so, in the case of the dwelling-place of the poor widow who owns the hens in the *Nun's Priest's Tale:* 'Ful sooty was hire bour and eek hir halle' [2832] is a witticism which plays on the difference between large medieval houses and one-room cottages – Knight 1973, p.213). This approach explores the unspoken premises of the texts. For example, reverting to a point mentioned under 'Source Study', the historical critic shows us how Duke Theseus tacitly contravenes a standard practice of medieval warfare in the *Knight's Tale* when he decides against ransoming his prisoners. Habitual medieval ransom procedures (from which Chaucer benefited himself when captured by the French) are clarified in a line of critics stretching back to Robertson, who thought Theseus conspicuously 'unmercenary' in disallowing ransom(1915, pp. 229–30). Incidentally, the controversial question whether the pilgrim Knight is himself more of an unworthy mercenary than the *General Prologue* asserts can only be resolved by studying documentary evidence to see how the contemporary nobility rated the battles in which the Knight participated (Keen 1983).

We can judge from other documents the extent to which the Prioress's portrait knowingly encapsulates formal complaints noted by bishops who inspected nunneries, even down to the detail of forbidden pet dogs, whose upkeep reduced the nuns' almsgiving and which fouled the cloisters into the bargain (Power 1924). Or we can learn about St Mary *Rouncivale*, an unpopular institution which the dubious Pardoner represents [*General Prologue*, 669–70). He is the more dubious if he is one of the Augustinian canons located there, because, long hair and all, he brazenly travesties their rules (Hamilton 1941). In the light of historical 'facts', says Hamilton, 'we perhaps can interpret Chaucer's pilgrim more nearly as . . . contemporaries must have done'. This is the traditional common-sense justification of historical research. Maybe it begs questions about the factuality of documentary sources and about our ability to avoid projecting our own mental constructs into history. But the sorry alternative to digging for 'facts' is to allow *Rouncivale* and much else to float by us while we read, as inscrutable and inert as a lump of debris in a river.

Some bracing, not to say sabre-rattling, views on Chaucer and the 'facts' of history have been proposed in recent sociological commentary. Of course, social structures *within* his poetry have been intermittently discussed in the past. Brewer's model analysis of 'Class-Distinction in Chaucer' unravelled a social complex ranging from the Parson's dogmatic assertion that 'God ordeyned that som folk sholde be moore heigh in estaat . . . and som folk moore lough', to the Wife of Bath's insistence in her tale that social rank is irrelevant to moral integrity – an idea with 'revolutionary' implications if it had been seriously taken as a call 'to organise social superiority on the basis of virtue' (1968, p.65). So far as aristocratic ideology is concerned, I have myself argued elsewhere that Chaucer so stresses *suffraunce*, and so deprives chivalric combat of charisma, as to criticise medieval society's traditional notion that knightly *worshipe* or honour depended upon a man's aggressive, retaliatory prowess (Blamires 1979).

Brewer maintained that the relationship between social configurations in Chaucer's poetry and the actual social situation was a problem best left to professional historians (1968, p.54). Such an arrangement is unattractive to radical critics, who seek to apply theories of the New Left to the *Tales*.

One of these theories concerns 'mediation, i.e. the process whereby literature restates problems of social conflict, even in those formal or aesthetic dimensions which previous criticism thought to be insulated from the author's environment. In the context of Richard II's reign, when the 'vertical' structure of state hierarchy seemed threatened by shifting 'horizontal' coalitions of baronial and mercantile groups as well as by peasant rebellion, Chaucer's reluctance to *rank* the pilgrims' viewpoints in the design of the *Tales* assumes social and political significance. In other words, by making us feel that truth is relative and by allowing speakers such as the Miller or Wife of Bath to pressurise established norms, Chaucer 'mediates' a climate of deteriorating hierarchical stability (Strohm 1979).

Modern French socio-literary theory can be used to suggest that the tales expose strains or 'fissures' in his ideological environment, and yet also close them off, cover them up (Knight 1980). When at the end the Parson returns us to orthodox morality, we see Chaucer reaching for an establishment reassurance that will close down the dynamic conflicts he has exposed. Likewise, even though the Miller and Reeve are allowed to register a vigorous, socially disruptive class-challenge against the *Knight's Tale*'s ethos of aristocratic order, Chaucer makes their disruptive fabliau world 'self-destruct'. The fact that a cuckolded carpenter breaks his arm, and a cuckolded miller is beaten up, is the poet's way of 'innoculating the texts against the perceived vigour of their class' (p.33).

These bracing suggestions lack persuasion if you suspect, with Brewer, that Chaucer's presentation of social status 'does not admit of broad mass groupings whose economic interests are identical within the group and opposed to other groups' (1968, p.62). Still, the claim that Chaucer both experiments with anti-authoritarian standpoints and retreats from such experiments is a refreshing feature in overlapping Marxist and feminist criticism.

Seen in these terms, the Pardoner challenges religious authority not simply because he touts bogus relics and pardons, but more profoundly because he makes us doubt whether *any* 'authoritative' discourse can be comfortably separated from the manipulative human agent who is expressing it – and who may, like the Pardoner, deploy chunks of Latin or rhetoric to keep his audience submissive (Aers 1980, pp. 89–93). Aers goes on to argue that the Host eventually attacks the Pardoner in an effort to restore the religious 'certainties and pieties' he has so threatened.

The Wife of Bath also challenges the supposedly impersonal authority of teachings: specifically, those which demoted women. In her prologue [707–10] she mischievously protests that clerical accusations against women characteristically get written by ecclesiasts (who in any case monopolised literacy) warped by the senile frustrated impotence of old age (Aers, pp. 83–4). On the other hand, both her prologue [823–5] and her tale [1255–6] seem finally to retreat into a compliant wifely 'kindness' to husbands, whereby the female challenge is 'feebly extinguished' (Knight 1980, p.34).

Moreover the Wife's challenge raises a further problem. The whole framework of thought within which women existed was, generally speaking, male-controlled. It was rooted in the cardinal principle of doctrine, that 'a womman sholde be subget to hire housbonde' [*Parson's Tale*, 929] – though the Parson qualifies this a little. Marriage was largely 'a transaction organised by males to serve economic and political ends, with the woman treated as a useful, child-bearing appendage' (Aers, p.143). No matter how energetically the Wife wants to fight, this framework of thought infiltrates her very attempt to rebel. Since, as has been shrewdly remarked, her identity is basically 'only an illusion maintained, as on a life-support system, by constant opposition to men' (Shoaf 1983, p.181), her challenge is confined to *turning the tables on men*. She seeks to wrest control of the money-chest from her men; 'markets' her sexuality, whereas men marketed women in marriage-making; throws anti-feminist diatribes in her husbands' faces; wants to appropriate sovereignty from males. But this doesn't *overturn* the tables. She doesn't so much assert Womanhood as reverse herself, in a sense, towards Man. She, and her creator, are locked into the 'difficulties of going beyond received paradigms and orthodoxies within received concepts and vocabulary' (Aers, pp. 147–50).

Put another way, this means the Wife of Bath is a male fantasy. In her is presented less a positive kind of female strength than a comic male 'nightmare': the woman 'who refuses to "know her place"'. We are switched uneasily between Chaucer's sympathetic insight into this woman's sense of lost youth and affection, and his glib use of her to 'exorcise the image of the overpowering female through comedy' (Diamond 1977, pp. 69–71).

It is interesting to note, finally, how feminist criticism perceives a retreat from 'socially subversive' pro-female positions in the *Wife of Bath's Tale* and *Franklin's Tale*. In the first a knight who rapes a girl is successively at the mercy of the queen and her ladies, then at the mercy of an old hag who alone knows the answer to their test question on which his life depends. The old witch 'wins' him as husband, subverting the romance cliché whereby a nobleman conventionally won the hand of a passive princess. So the tale's casually domineering hero tastes what it was to be, like medieval women in life (or idealised females in romance), a marital pawn or prize (Haskell 1978, pp. 10–12). Yet, since the hag mutates at the conclusion into a submissive beauty, this challenge to masculine supremacy fades. Domineering males need not worry, for 'even witches will capitulate . . . if they are given some token respect' (Diamond, p.73).

The same rhythm is found in the *Franklin's Tale*. There is here a fine-sounding initial definition of the loving sensitivity in Dorigen and Arveragus's relationship – though from a feminist viewpoint it is already compromised by the couple's agreement that Arveragus shall have the *name of soveraynetee* in public [751–2]. Later, when Dorigen is in despair over the crisis of her commitment to adultery with squire Aurelius, her husband exercises male prerogative, taking her decision for her. If the Franklin reflects at first Chaucer's 'utopian' aspiration to transcend the current power-structure of marriage, Dorigen's emotional dependence in that moment of crisis makes for a collapse back into the old hierarchy (Aers, pp. 160–9). How much she is in fact conditioned by her culture seems anyway to emerge in the near-brutal candour with which she envisages that her husband 'hath hir body whan so that hym liketh' [1003–5].

On the whole Dorigen's role only contributes to an image of *suffering* woman enshrined elsewhere in tales such as the Clerk's. Perhaps in Chaucer's world women have little choice 'but to suffer, and therefore their greatest virtue lies in suffering well' (Diamond, p.74). If so, it needs to be added that this female function of suffering is also represented by Chaucer as a profoundly humane quality which we might better term calm benignity, or forgiving tolerance. In his *Tale of Melibee* a woman's unrestrained tongue (which in other contexts characterises the stock 'jangling' wife of medieval satire) becomes an instrument of that kind of tolerance. A nobleman's wife quietly but resolutely induces her aggressive husband to soften his anger against enemies who have raided his home. In assigning this tale to himself, Chaucer conceivably registers a personal wish that more of his male contemporaries would subdue their belligerent instincts and emulate the *suffraunce* such a woman displays.

Dramatic or psychological readings

As we have just seen, the Franklin and Wife of Bath appear to dispossess males of their *maistrie* in only a fleeting and token way. Let us glance at the psychological (as distinct from the sociological) repercussions of this.

If Chaucer implies that women would like 'a *token* submission on the part of the husband', but having gained *maistrie* 'they want not to exercise it', is he projecting 'an ambivalent wish typical of human nature, and as true of men as of women'? Is he suggesting that 'we want to be dependent and independent both . . . that neither men nor women fully know what they want and most often want it both ways' (Howard 1976, pp. 254–5)? These questions exemplify critical engagement with the psychology of 'human nature' in Chaucer. It is hardly controversial to talk of his interest in human nature. However, debate begins as soon as we begin to ask how, in terms of characterisation, the tales explore that interest.

I shall approach this obliquely by mentioning a matter of neglect in the climax of the *Wife of Bath's Tale*. Here a young nobleman is brought willy-nilly to bed with the ugly old peasant dame who has claimed him in marriage. Naturally he writhes on the sheets, distraught with parodic honeymoon frigidity while his grizzled bedmate lies smiling next to him [1083–6]. Neither seems to move from the bed's tense intimacy during her ensuing harangue, or 'pillow lecture'. At the woman's moment of magic transformation, there is suddenly a 'curtyn' which the nobleman must 'cast up' to appreciate her beauty [1239–49]. Presumably it is a curtain hung around the bed: in the contemporary romance *Sir Gawain and the Green Knight*, line 1185, Gawain momentarily 'caught up' the corner of such a curtain to watch from his bed a lady entering his room. Chaucer's nobleman has to let in light (sunlight? moonlight? torchlight?) to view his transformed bride. We realise that Chaucer has hardly supplied any circumstantial detail. It is even possible that, in order to stiffen the shock of revelation, the poet has silently catapulted the writhing youth right out of the bed, so that he must 'cast up the curtain' from *outside* – as does Sir Gawain's visitor at line 1192 of the romance – to behold the occupant.

Other examples would confirm that Chaucer's attention to spatial context is sometimes cavalier (strange things happen to a grove in the *Knight's Tale*) and generally not fully naturalistic. Should we therefore also expect Chaucer's characterisation to show a partial naturalism, rather than the kind of integrated illusion of human personality cultivated in more recent literature? Many critics think so (e.g. Jordan 1962, 1967). On the other hand Chaucer is sometimes distinctly more 'modern' in creating naturalistic characters than he is in modelling narrative background. Comparison with the period's visual arts is interesting in this respect because they often display a clash of styles – between a 'flat, two-dimensional' unnaturalistic backdrop, and human figures who are contrastingly 'solid, substantial, three-dimensional' (Spearing 1972, pp. 104–5).

Spearing offers this comparison in relation to the *Clerk's Tale*, which has been thought a classic hybrid in the different sense that it invites us both to view its heroine Griselda as a 'flat' emblem of undeviating Christian obedience to the Creator *and* to side with her emotionally as a woman tormented by the wilful sadism of her husband Walter (Bronson 1960, pp. 103–15).

It is a logical conclusion that the tales therefore embody a dynamic transitional approach to literary characterisation whereby naturalistic experiment jostles with the older modes of stereotyping that we noted in the section 'Retrieving Literary Conventions'. This requires of us a corresponding flexibility of response. Thus, although Walter's machinations against Griselda (determined by the received shape of the story) make his behaviour as a typecast 'Tester' appear implausible, he may be said to melodramatise 'a pattern . . . in some real-life marriages, in which cruelty on one side is met with submission on the other, and that in turn provokes still greater cruelty on the first' (Spearing 1972, p.97). In that case the tale becomes partly a psychological study of Walter's obsession with pushing his wife to the limits of obedience, no less than the *Canon's Yeoman's Tale* appears to explore the psychology of obsession in the way its speaker pores morbidly over the jargon, chicanery and hypnotism of alchemy.

Of course the tales activate our psychologising instincts above all by their implicit invitation to experience the pilgrim teller in the tale. Kittredge inspired generations of readers with the idea that the tales are essentially 'long speeches expressing . . . the characters' of each pilgrim; that the pilgrims are the 'dramatis personae' in a grand 'Human Comedy'; and that Chaucer meant to 'seize the moment of intensest self-revelation' for each of them (1915, pp. 154–5, 179). Years later readers were still being told that 'the proper context for a given story consists primarily of the individual traits and dramatic purposes of the Pilgrim telling that story' (Lumiansky 1955, p.4).

Clearly Chaucer did begin to play a complex literary game, in which he saw the potential for vigorous interaction between the tales, the *Prologue* descriptions, and colourful between-tales repartee. The question is, did he play this game as avidly as the dramatic critics want him to? Does the Monk tell dour tragedies to punish the Host for presuming to joke about his virility, or again because, as one who usurps the aristocratic lifestyle, he seeks to match the pilgrim Knight's philosophical tragedy? Does the Nun's Priest's story of a hen-circled cockerel purge the speaker's sense of suffocation amidst a cloisterful of nuns? Such inquiries slip easily into subjective interpretation. Many critics think Chaucer only sporadically moulded tales with an eye to their speakers: so we should beware of being 'goaded', by the surface *un*suitability of some tales to their tellers, into sophisticated psychological hypotheses (Bronson 1960, pp. 71–9). Even the most strikingly apt tales, according to Muscatine, will not evince the kind of verbal individualisation which distinguishes one character from another in drama proper. In mediating between teller and tale, Chaucer 'sought not an idiomatic but a tonal and attitudinal relationship'. He would not have comprehensively modified his narrative skills 'merely to make a story sound as if such and such a character were actually telling it' (1957, p.172).

Given that the Wife of Bath and Pardoner are provided with self-revealing monologues, they at least would appear ripe for intensive psychological analysis. They are and they aren't. The *Wife of Bath's Prologue* brilliantly projects a compelling semblance of personality out of Chaucer's piecemeal literary borrowings. But her personality has loose ends which defeat character-study. For example, in denouncing her fourth husband as an adulterer she is pleased to report that she made him fry in his own grease by pretending to take lovers herself, though *not* to the point of sex itself, 'Nat of my body, in no foul manere' [481–8]. How do we reconcile this puritan note with what she otherwise says about her appetite for sexual adventure, so ungovernable that she 'koude noght withdrawe' her 'chambre of Venus from a good felawe' whenever one was handy [615–26]? To salvage consistency we should have to conjecture that the prurience is meant in jest; or that she is deceiving herself regarding that period of her life (Owen 1977, pp. 149–50); or, alternatively, that the prurience hints at a 'real' Alisoun mostly hidden behind the mask of a Scarlet Woman.

If we manage to solve such discrepancies, critical sleight of hand is again required to dovetail the strenuously moral 'pillow lecture' in Alisoun's tale with the psyche she has revealed in her prologue (Slade, in Anderson, *Casebook*, pp. 168–70). Incidentally, let us note at this stage that the *Wife of Bath's Tale* is among those which have attracted *psychoanalytic* attention: i.e. study of the 'central fantasy' informing the text. The story's opening rape and its concluding prospect of cross-generation

sex involve 'some sense of taboos broken'. Like the Wife of Bath
herself, the old crone expresses 'the giving, outpouring quality
of woman' because she gives away the secret of what women
desire. And at the very core of the narrative we reach an
adolescent fantasy which (it is claimed) precedes all other
critical exposition: 'if I am phallically aggressive and do not
submit to my mother, she will castrate me' (Holland 1967).
The Pardoner excites equally breathtaking psychoanalysis,
since by any standards he is fascinatingly repellent. Howard,
while abstaining from outright castration-fantasies, thinks him
a manic figure, 'sexually anomalous, hermaphroditic,
menacing, contradictory'. The Pardoner has a compulsive need
to exercise power over the victims of his frauds so that he can
prevent them from deriding his feminoid appearance. He is a
study in alienated resentment, in 'the obsessional or
psychopathic character' (1976, pp. 339–76). Howard argues
that this modern-sounding diagnosis does not conflict with the
text's relation to the medieval doctrine of sin, though he
certainly does de-emphasise an influential theological
interpretation of the Pardoner as a 'Scriptural Eunuch' (Miller
1955).

There is again a problem of consistency. When the Pardoner
unexpectedly crowns his tale with a blandly pious protestation
that *Christ's* pardon is what really matters, then proceeds with
an amazing last-ditch attempt to impose his 'sacred' relics on
the pilgrims (who have previously heard how fraudulent they
are), he creates a crux for Chaucer criticism. Does Chaucer
present these manoeuvres as convolutions of the man's
mocking bravado? What about Bronson's nuts-and-bolts
hypothesis that the poet conceived of the Pardoner's opening
self-revelations *after* he had written the rest, failing to iron out
the discrepancy this generated at the end (1960, pp. 80–7)?

Maybe after all consistency didn't matter so much to
Chaucer – he just seized an opportunity to develop a hint in *The
Romance of the Rose* where the analogous hypocrite ('False
Seeming') crowns his self-revelations by saying he dare not lie
to his present audience, but would certainly try to trick them if
he felt that they could be duped (Muscatine 1972, pp. 116–18).
In developing this, Chaucer perhaps wanted to crush the
Pardoner, both by intruding the primacy of Christ's pardon
and by engineering a provocative piece of salesmanship which

would incite the Host's retaliation. That is to say, the autonomy of the Pardoner's character is compromised by the poet's intervention.

We have to remember that *Chaucer is writing the speakers*. Theoretically this produces two voices in a tale. Burlin talks of the *Franklin's Tale* as 'the work of two creators, of Chaucer and Chaucer's Franklin' (in Anderson, *Casebook*, p.199). In his view the poet lurks in the rear. In the foreground the Franklin betrays himself as a narrator who, not being to the manner born in the *gentil* class, remains self-consciously uncomfortable with the rhetoric and the behaviour he deems proper to his *gentil* story. One example of his unease occurs when he describes Dorigen's distress while her husband is away, weeping and sighing 'As doon thise noble wyves whan hem liketh. / She moorneth, waketh, wayleth, fasteth, pleyneth' [817–9]. For Burlin, this conveys the Franklin's pragmatic suspicion that high-born ladies indulge in extravagant displays of emotion which are 'the prerogative of an idle class' (Anderson, *Casebook*, pp. 195–6).

Other scholars, thinking of similar sentiment-puncturing lines in Chaucer's *Troilus*, would detect here not the Franklin's voice but a specimen of the *poet's* celebrated 'ambiguity of tone' (Mann 1982, pp. 141–2). Mann suggests that the effect in this case is to impose on Dorigen's emotion an amused – but not unsympathetic – sense of how it would look when time has healed her grief. But our present concern is to realise how Chaucer's authorial attitudes invade the pilgrim storytellers more extensively than Burlin implies. At any moment Chaucer may override the pilgrim speaker, for instance 'with a display of witty erudition he has chosen to discuss through the medium' of that speaker (Burnley 1983, p.170). He may, as Howard puts it, 'unimpersonate' amidst his 'impersonation' of a pilgrim (1976, p. 231).

The reader therefore confronts a task of the utmost delicacy, attempting to decide which bits of the narrative cake should be allocated to the pilgrim character and which to the author. Unless, that is, we up-end this entire debate with a bomb manufactured according to the principles of recent French literary theorists such as Derrida. *Avant-garde* theory holds that we should stop thinking about *external* speakers (whether pilgrims or poet) because in the *Tales* 'there is nobody there,

there is only the text'. It is the text which creates a 'voice', not vice-versa. The tales 'concentrate not on the way pre-existing people create language but on the way language creates people' (Leicester 1980). Whether this will prove a Waterloo in Chaucer criticism is not yet clear. The dynamite is a little disappointing in its practical effects. The *General Prologue* turns out to be a text which creates 'a speaker who is not giving too much of himself away', and we shall only discover the poet's voice by assimilating the successive voices which the tales create: hardly earth-shattering suggestions.

In 1974 it seemed that 'the old dramatic view of the poem' still had 'life in it' (Anderson, *Casebook*, p.15). Given the combination of the design of the *Tales* and our incorrigible thirst for personality in poetry, I doubt readers will ever stop puzzling over the teller in the tale, whether they work from the pilgrim to the narrative or from the text back to the 'voice' that the text creates. And, since some of the early manuscripts placed an illuminated picture of the pilgrim at the head of each tale, we are not without historical warrant for a 'dramatic' reading.

Varieties of textual analysis

For most readers, 'textual analysis' means that technique of close reading broadly associated with New Criticism. We shall leave aside specialised sub-categories, but one problem of terminology is unavoidable. By New Criticism we mean '(Old) New Criticism', characteristic of much literary study from the 1940s to the 1960s. Since then there have been waves of Brand New Critical theory – usually identified by generic titles such as 'Structuralism'.

As late as 1963, Payne felt there had been too little close verbal analysis of Chaucer (p.2). But by 1967 Holland was championing his psychoanalytical approach to the *Wife of Bath's Tale* against the 'overly intellectual, even sterile' methods of New Criticism (p.280). And in 1972 Muscatine proclaimed that New Critical concentration exclusively on the text at the expense of historical or cultural context had 'reached a dead end' (p.4). To judge from these dates, close reading of Chaucer had only nine years in which to arrive, go sterile, and die. The burial was premature. In 1973 nobody, according to Knight, had even yet elucidated 'the detailed working' of Chaucer's poetry (p.xiii): Knight's book, like many since, proves that this approach speaks volubly in its grave.

Brand New Critical theory is fragmented at present into a babel of rival tongues in a perpetual crisis of conflict. Until it stabilises, one must suppose that, for most students, the heritage of New Criticism will remain familiar, something only to be exterminated with painful effort. So I shall not labour its characteristics: its stringent analysis of stylistic nuance, metrical subtlety, wordplay and levels of diction, point of view, imagery, ambiguities, structured oppositions – and, above all, its concern to make every part of the textual fabric participate in a comprehensive self-sufficient unity.

We can sample only a tiny fraction of close readings. Knight himself scrutinises the effect of each twist of rhetoric in the *Tales;* he strains to articulate nuances of diction ('ornate', 'learned', 'blunt', 'direct'); and he riskily attributes qualities to the syntactical movement of the verse ('slack', 'clipped', 'aggressive', etc.). Meticulous attention to syntax is also exemplified in Spearing's account of the *Franklin's Tale.* When squire Aurelius must inform Dorigen that the 'impossible' task upon which her favours depend is performed, Spearing shows how his speech [1311–38] begins as a composed and formal supplication expressing the courtly lover's conventional *drede.* But the formality is a cover for his nervous excitement, which 'breaks through the lucid rhetorical structure' as he 'loses himself in parentheses', unable to spell out that the rocks guaranteeing her loyalty to her husband have disappeared (1966, pp. 44–5).

Other practitioners continued to wield the 'tools' of New Criticism in the 1970s. Owen, for instance, demonstrates Chaucer's clever use of rhyme; and he exercises onomatopoeic analysis, as in the suggestion that line 151 of the *General Prologue* describing the Prioress ('Ful semyly hir wympul pynched was') communicates the lady's 'prim surfaces' through its 'labials and close front vowels' (1977, p.60). Critics of another persuasion will frequently be found semi-New-Critical. Kean emphasises Chaucer's skill in timing and placing nonchalant give-away words, such as the quietly suggestive 'faire' in a *Prologue* couplet [233–4] about the Friar's stock of 'knyves / And pynnes, for to yeven faire wyves' (1972, pp. 80–1).

We might mention here an early, classic study which composes the *Prologue's* parts into a triumphant unity (Hoffman 1954, in Anderson, *Casebook*). Hoffman observes that the text opens with a movement from springtime quickening (moisture impregnating the earth; renewed human energy) to specific pilgrimage: that is, from an archetype of 'secular' regenerative love towards a shrine typifying restorative spiritual love. This sets up a paradigm, with 'Saint Venus' as alternative to, yet ultimately subject to, 'Saint Thomas'. Into this paradigm can be locked all the pilgrims, whether as individuals (the Prioress) or as pairs (Knight–Squire, and Summoner–Pardoner too, because they are defective instruments of God's summoning and God's pardoning whose duet 'Com hider, love, to me!' betrays their need for spiritual *amor* amidst their debasement of it).

No doubt the Friar's 'knyves' for pretty housewives would contribute to such a 'unity'. Literally, they epitomise the tactical free gift. The fifteenth-century pilgrim Margery Kempe recalls a friar who gave her 'a peyr of knyvys in tokyn that he wolde standyn wyth hir in Goddys cawse'. But it is quite possible that Friar Huberd's knives express a phallic image (Ross 1972, pp. 126–7) confirming that, for him too, St Venus blocks out St Thomas.

New Criticism has assiduously examined each tale for patterns of symbolism and of imagery (Owen 1953; Richardson 1970). If labials and close front vowels now look somewhat outmoded, imagery flourishes still. Kolve, for example, argues that the portrait of Alisoun in the *Miller's Tale* [3233ff.] oscillates between images projecting her 'free' and 'untamed' animal nature, and images of confinement (fastened brooch, apron, shoes laced high on her legs) which project her old husband's foolish attempt to cage up her friskiness (1984, pp. 162–3).

By contrast, Brand New Critical ideas flood through another critic's ingenious commentary on coin-imagery in Chaucer. He identifies a precedent for *avant-garde* theories on the problem of meaning in language, in a medieval philosopher's comparison between bits of metal coined to circulate as the price-equivalent of specific things, and 'sounds' that are coined into words having specific current significances (Shoaf 1983, pp. 8–11). A poet who circulates the 'coinage' of words has to avoid contaminating language with a 'false imprint' for self-seeking ends. One ramification of this complex point is that Chaucer shows how individuals, like lecherous old January in the *Merchant's Tale*, try to 'falsify' other people in terms of their own egotistical impulses (pp. 185–209). Shoaf describes January as a counterfeiter in the sense that January wants to manufacture, or coin, some girl into the sexually compliant wife of his dreams – indeed, in January's own idiom, to mould some 'yong thyng' just as men shape 'warm wex' with their hands [1429–30]. He chooses May on this basis. But she turns out far too pliable, only too receptive to the emotions of a household squire whose 'impression' cuts into her heart [1977–81]. Moreover, January 'the false coiner' paradoxically grows so infatuated with this wife he had intended to mould that she becomes 'depe enprented' in his 'thoght' [2178].

At this point we encounter a problem which besets textual analysis generally. Can Chaucer's language-use genuinely sustain, in this instance, Shoaf's 'coinage' interpretation? According to another scholar, the phraseology of *impressiounes* engraved upon thoughts or hearts belongs essentially to a cluster of medieval language concerning the mechanism of human perception. In that language, external *ymages* were considered to be 'printed' into the mind like letters incised in wax; a person's *ymaginacioun* could summon up these engraved images at will. The minds of Chaucer's lovers are often so forcefully etched with the partner's image that rational control over the image fails, and *fantasies* of emotion take over (Burnley 1979, pp. 99–115). It appears that 'coinage' implications in the *Merchant's Tale* might be rather marginal to the Chaucerian architecture of language within which Burnley locates such diction of 'imprinting'.

As Burnley says, we have to determine what meanings are *possible* in Chaucer's poetry if we are to construct a historically plausible interpretation (p.3). A card-carrying New Critic might want to isolate the text from its social–historical context; yet he must admit the need to 'know what the poem's words would have meant to their original readers' (Eagleton 1983, p.48). It is a crucial admission. Close analysis of the *Tales* faces from the start the difficulty of judging what overtones were present in words in Chaucer's time. And a quest for overtones drives us back to the historical culture (e.g. medieval ideas about *impressiounes* on the mind) which determines them.

To reconstruct the overtones – to gauge the phallic possibility in the Friar's knives and so forth – we must, ideally, ponder the whole recorded life of words in the period's writings. In the *Miller's Tale*, sinuous Alisoun is compared to a weasel [3234]. Is there an overtone of sexual mobility, deriving from an observation in medieval animal lore that the weasel 'moves with subtle cunning from one part of the house to another so that it lies each night in a different lair' (Richardson 1970, p. 163)? Again, what are the stylistic overtones of 'licour', a word used for spring rain in the third line of the *General Prologue?* We shall easily suppose it a piece of elevated diction, but there is linguistic evidence to the contrary (Blake 1977, p. 91). There is even, in Blake's view, evidence for saying that the range of verbal overtone available to medieval poets was severely restricted (pp. 80–90).

Mindful of such considerations, the best New Critics have always reckoned with the framework of medieval linguistic usage. The old mirage of a Berlin Wall dividing 'language' scholars from 'literary critics' was dispelled by Donaldson (1950, in Anderson, *Casebook*). He engagingly combined New Critical flair with philological precision in his discussion of words in the *Miller's Tale* which mischievously parody phraseology in popular vernacular romance and love-song.

Brewer is another critic who has recruited traditional philology into the service of modern modes of analysis. For instance, he discusses the word 'sad' used insistently to define Griselda's behaviour in the *Clerk's Tale*. Emphasising the word's pervasive medieval meaning, 'self-restraint/sobriety/constancy', he exhaustively investigates what other words are associated with it in that tale and in Chaucer's whole work. In the process, he finds confirmation of a hypothesis that Chaucer's style is fundamentally 'metonymic' – a term borrowed from modern linguistics to indicate a sideways method of associating ideas rather than a 'metaphorical' method which compacts ideas together (1974, pp. 44-51).

We have been talking so far as if the text, with its problematic stylistic overtones, were reliably authorial. Not least of the analyst's headaches is that it isn't. The tales we read in standard editions are printed reconstructions. They have decided for us what Chaucer 'really wrote' wherever the medieval manuscripts show disagreement from one scribe's rendering to another's. Life is perhaps too short for the ordinary reader to agonise over this. But it may be important to remember that the printed text has also begun to control our interpretation by substituting the fastidious resources of modern punctuation for the indiscriminate-looking mass of oblique strokes which was mostly what chopped up verse-paragraphs in the manuscripts. Consider this notorious couplet describing the Wife of Bath:

> She was a worthy womman / al hir lyue
> Housbondes at chirche dore / she hadde fyue
>
> [*General Prologue*, 459–60]

That is how it appears in the 'Hengwrt' manuscript, which is available in reproduction and well worth inspection if one has the chance (Ruggiers 1979). As Donaldson points out, in the absence of punctuation the relationship between the first line and the second, though hinted by rhyme, remains inscrutable. A modern semicolon after 'lyue' would insinuate a teasing link between the Wife's 'worthiness' and her husband-consumption; but innuendo fades if you put a full-stop there instead (1974, pp.87–8).

Retreating from these unnerving textual conundrums, we only encounter another hurdle for New Criticism, i.e. general uncertainty about the intended *order* of the tales. It is a subject of byzantine complexity. Only certain groups of tales emerge as moderately stable authorial entities. These groups themselves were shuffled around each other in different manuscripts, like documents in a loose file, in ways that pose problems for inter-tale theories such as Kittredge's popular claim that there is an extended 'Discussion of Marriage' (1912, in Anderson, *Casebook)*. Strictly speaking, New Critical study of large-scale organisation has to be confined within the 'stable' groups. Some groups (e.g. Knight–Miller–Reeve) have long been surveyed as broader structures. New Critical perseverance has gradually discovered subtle joinery in other, sometimes less 'stable', groups. For example, an image of 'sweat' seems to link the *Second Nun's Tale* with the *Canon's Yeoman's Prologue*. In the first, a female Christian martyr miraculously stays sweatless while tortured in a boiling bath; in the second, an alchemist sweats profusely under the compulsion of his headlong quest for gold.

The case for inter-tale structures has been pursued to its limits by Cooper (1983). However, the case for 'deep structures' within the entire work (taking up aspects of Structuralist theory we noted at the end of the 'Source Study' section) is open for investigation. Mann is a leading investigator. Discussing the *Franklin's Tale*, she identifies the process of change or *aventure* as its governing concept: only by actively 'surrendering' to the impetus of change do the tale's characters release new energies. But the paradox that 'patience conquers' extends far beyond this one story: it is in fact 'at the heart of the *Canterbury Tales*' (1982).

Among other things, Mann here begins to nudge us away from standard New Critical diagnosis of Chaucer's ambiguity of tone, of his ability to induce both approval and disapproval in the reader (p.142). The New Critical era has indeed been the heyday of the ironical Chaucer, the ambivalent Chaucer, whose tales hold multifarious responses to life in artful equipoise. It has been the era of Donaldson's Chaucer – the dualistic poet who arranges for the 'moralist' part of himself 'to define austerely *what ought to be*' even while his humane *alter ego* goes on 'affirming affectionately *what is*' (1954, in Anderson, *Casebook*, p.103; emphasis added). If we are now, finally, striking away from this exhaustively cultivated New Critical terrain and crossing the Rubicon, it would nevertheless require a guide with better binoculars than mine to declare confidently just which critical routes hold most promise on the other side.

Part Two
Appraisal

Introduction

THE FOLLOWING appraisal of the *Canterbury Tales* is not a specimen of any clear-cut 'X' or 'Y' sectarian approach. It is best characterised through a process of partial elimination, which leaves room for a broadly based (but not infinitely elastic) reading, and thereby acknowledges the unsectarian multifaceted quality of Chaucer's writing. Here is a clue already: for I should certainly favour the proposition that Chaucer's method 'is to show an aspect of truth, criticise it, suggest its partiality, set up a counter-truth ... never quite settle, never give a conclusive answer' (Whittock 1968, p.294).

A famous example of the poet's probable inconclusiveness occurs in the *General Prologue* description of the Franklin [331–60]. In his house 'it snewed ... of mete and drynke'. Himself partial to expensively sauced cuisine and to a morning 'sop in wyn', the Franklin aims to 'lyven in delit', in the Epicurean belief that bodily pleasure is the ultimate 'felicitee'. In the next breath we are told that he was a 'Seint Julian' in his locality.

We are caught in a trap here. Other perspectives in the *Tales* might make us doubt the moral credibility of a man associated (however enthusiastically) with consumable 'deyntees'. The Nun's Priest affectionately presents a widow who radiates robust health on an enforced slender diet that is the reverse of the Franklin's. Elsewhere we find that, from a preacher's viewpoint, a devotee of 'deyntee mete and drynke' is spiritually dead [*Pardoner's Tale*, 517–48]: and it is notable that Chaucer's favourite philosopher, Boethius, strenuously upholds an idea of *felicitee* that explicitly transcends Epicurean pleasure-seeking.

Nevertheless, the Franklin represents a literary trap, in two ways. First, no verdict is expressed on his Epicureanism. Contrast the decisive implications in a Boccaccio story where a rich citizen imprudently remarks that his cellar boasts a wine so superb that Christ would have delighted in it. For this innocuous 'blasphemy' he is interrogated by ecclesiastical authorities as severely as if he were actually an 'Epicurean who

47

denied the immortality of the soul' (*Decameron*, I.6). Boccaccio makes clear that a committed Epicurean would be beyond the pale. Chaucer does not. Second, if we *do* infer that the Franklin is dangerously materialistic, this judgement is immediately unsettled by his role as a St Julian, because Julian was legendary for keeping open house to look after the poor and sick.

Chaucer's description tangles up the amiable gourmet with the saint in a challengingly inconclusive way. But this reading, it should be noted, arises from a New Critical emphasis largely on the description's internal structure, suppressing external factors which might enter into either a Marxist or an allegorical approach. Those approaches would converge in this instance towards a hostile and in my view over-simplified reading of the Franklin, as a hedonistic member of the 'landed gentry' who banquets the rich with (sinful) delicacies accumulated by exploiting the very peasants to whom he can then condescend as their 'St Julian'.

Underlying assumptions in my 'Appraisal' may be further disclosed with reference to the Wife of Bath. In the section 'Medieval intellectual contexts' we saw how an allegorical critic would use doctrinal commentary to brand her a 'hopelessly carnal' person because she did not fathom what, according to medieval theologians, Christ meant when he rebuked the Samaritan woman at the well concerning her present partner. I should prefer to stress the wording of an allusion to this biblical episode, in a pro-chastity treatise by St Jerome which Chaucer is plundering in the *Wife of Bath's Prologue*. St Jerome argues,

> it is better to know a single husband, though he be a second or third, than to have many paramours: that is, it is more tolerable for a woman to prostitute herself to one man than to many. At all events this is so *if* the Samaritan woman in John's Gospel who said that she had her sixth [?] husband was reproved by the Lord *because* he was not her husband. (Miller 1977, pp. 424–5; emphasis and query added).

Chaucer simply takes up from that *if*–clause a note of uncertainty for the Wife to develop, since she aims to question whether God's 'expres word' [61] ever prohibits remarriage.

Furthermore, it seems unnecessary to admit any 'allegorical' element, beyond what the Bible itself furnishes by having Christ present himself to the Samaritan woman as a source of 'living water' which will quench her spiritual, as opposed to bodily, thirst (John 4:10–14). The language of 'refreshment' here catches Chaucer's attention. It links up with the Wife's preceding reference to Christ at the Canaan wedding (where he turned water into wine), and it inaugurates a pattern of imagery. The Wife goes into raptures over the prospect of being sexually 'refresshed' as often as Solomon was by his multitude of 'wyves' [35–8]. She concedes that Christ is the 'welle' of perfection [107]. But, mischievously noting that he 'refresshed' a multitude of 5000 with 'barly-breed', she is happy to grade herself as a commonplace barley-loaf female offered for mass consumption rather than as the select white bread of female chastity [142–6 (again manipulating Jerome: Miller, p.418)]. Then she gives another witty twist to the image when she squashes the Pardoner for presuming to interrupt her. She declares she will now open a 'tonne' (cask) containing a brew of enough marital bitterness to put him off the idea of taking a 'sippe' of marriage for good [163–78].

Where does this reading locate us? It respects primary sources (St Jerome; the Bible) but does not admit influence from allegorising medieval biblical commentaries. We recognise the Wife's parody of spiritual 'refreshment', but we stress the audacious, sparkling *play of mind* with which that parody complicates our response: is she, in her own bodily way, trying to imitate the principle of generosity which makes Christ a well-spring of nourishment for the soul? We are also subordinating psychological considerations, and conducting a New Critical analysis of a nucleus of imagery vividly adapted from its sources. Yet we should have to qualify that by noting that this imagery is only intermittent in the remainder of the *Wife of Bath's Prologue*. For all his subtlety with imagery, Chaucer is apparently not committed to generating an entire structure organically around it.

I have just spoken of the 'play of mind' in the poetry. Without demeaning Chaucer's emotional vibrancy, it seems that to appreciate the Wife of Bath we need a taste for witty ingenuity, a taste for comically resonant and even breathtaking exploration of topics (e.g. promiscuity) with which in other contexts we might engage more solemnly. It so happens that an audience possessing something like this taste occurs within the fiction, in the *Summoner's Tale* [2162–294]. There a friar, for good reason, receives the insult of a monstrous fart. The fart constitutes the 'present' which a villager has promised him on condition that he will divide it among his colleagues. The friar rushes in a towering rage to report this 'blasphemy' at the manor house. But his pious indignation is withered by the urbane response of the manorial family to his tale. It is the wit of the fart-division problem that absorbs their imagination. When a squire named Jankyn contrives to solve this problem, he is complimented by the entire household for his 'subtiltee / And heigh wit' [2290–1].

Taking a hint from Kean, who suggests (1972, pp.88–90) that this manorial audience has the kind of taste for 'virtuosity' which Chaucer wants readers to bring to his comic tales, I would support a 'Jankyn approach' to the *Tales* as a whole. This does not entail ignoring the serious themes they express. (It is noteworthy that the lord of the manor urges patience upon the apoplectic friar, and thus incidentally confirms that the adage 'Patience conquers' is – as we saw in the last section – ingrained in the *Tales'* wisdom). But it does entail our using supple resources of 'subtiltee and heigh wit' to track Chaucer's fertile play of mind.

Having said that, the Jankyn response is actually a little too suave, and the manorial audience too narrowly unanimous in commending such suavity, for us to rest wholly content with their approach. Chaucer knows that our responses will be mixed, just as among the pilgrims 'diverse folk diversely they seyde' in the aftermath of the *Miller's Tale* [*Reeve's Prologue*, 3857]. More than that, the tales seem calculated to raise questions about the processes by which an author creates, and an audience fashions its approaches to, narrative. Debate on the meaning of his story-matter may be said to begin within the poet's own work. In the next section we shall consider just how that happens.

Chaucer, authorship and truth

In the *Pardoner's Tale*, a sequence of exclamations beginning 'O cursed synne of alle cursednesse!' condemning homicide, gluttony, and so on [895f.] prompts one medieval scribe to write 'Auctor' in the margin. In another manuscript a scribe adds 'Auctor' next to a paragraph in the *Merchant's Tale* proclaiming the fickleness of Chance: 'O sodeyn hap! o thou Fortune unstable!' [2057f.].

In these particular instances the scribes probably mean to signal to us that the *Auctor* (author) is developing from his narrative a memorable piece of edifying wisdom, which we should as it were read in italics. The portentous quality of the rhetoric is obvious in any case, but we are not as familiar as the scribes were with an assumption that stories relay *auctoritee:* i.e. that inherited stories communicate the 'authority' of past wisdom, and that the poet ideally preserves or reinforces the wisdom inherent in a story as he transmits it. A story's 'authority' derived in fact from considerations such as (a) its antiquity, (b) its association with some celebrated past writer, and (c) its continuing capacity to exemplify general truths (e.g. 'Fortune is fickle').

It follows that the medieval poet was theoretically rather a passive instrument, reverentially channelling 'authoritative' narrative structures. Although factor (c) gave him some elbow-room, it was room not so much for self-expression as for disclosing new layers of impersonal truth that the narrative might support. Wherever he most conspicuously articulated such a 'truth', he would most inspire awe as an *Auctor* – a beacon of *auctoritee* – himself.

In practice, the majority of story-collections in the Middle Ages used narrative to propound moral truths (Cooper 1983, pp.8–55). Readers must have *expected* stories to yield edifying lessons. To modern eyes, the lessons sometimes seem bizarre; they seem to abuse the stories to which they are attached, by forcing moral significance across them. I shall argue that Chaucer actually recognised narrative's vulnerability to abuse in his culture (indeed in any culture), and that he sought to express this recognition creatively within the design of *The Canterbury Tales.*

Let us first ask what questions about authorship are raised in his earlier poetry. Like many poets of the time, he was attracted to the venerable story of Troy, but realised also the controversial nature of 'authorities' concerning that story. Homer was one great *Auctor*, yet there were those who claimed that through patriotic bias he 'made lyes . . . And was to Grekes favorable' [*House of Fam*, 1475–80]. For Chaucer the love-poet, this problem of divergent authorities became most worrying in relation to that classic of passion and betrayal following on from the fall of Troy – the short-lived love affair between Dido and Aeneas at Carthage. In a nutshell, Virgil's account insisted that Aeneas was duty-bound to abandon the too-infatuated Dido because of his exalted mission to found Rome. Ovid, however, took Dido's side: she was a loyal tragic heroine whose emotions were trifled with by a philandering visitor.

Which authority on Dido was Chaucer to transmit? The 'truths' derivable from her story would differ according to his choice. In the event he tried in *The House of Fame* to blend both accounts, though temperamentally perhaps inclining towards Ovidian sympathy for Dido. He has her forecast that her reputation will be torn to shreds, so to speak, by the Virgilian press; she'll become a simplified example of foolish passion, denigrated 'over al thys lond, on every tonge' [345–60]. Broadly, Chaucer implies that the *auctoritee* of old books holds no guarantee of impersonality or impartiality. Time-honoured story seems subject to the distorting lens of the writer transmitting it, no less than a piece of news heard on the street is subject to the fallibility of those who pass it along: for no one carries 'tidynges' a hundred steps without exercising the pleasurable human faculty of exaggeration [2059–67]. Moreover, literature does not escape the distortion-process by professing to rely on the creative imagination rather than on inherited writings. In *The House of Fame* Chaucer imagines himself taking an intergalactical voyage, only to discover that his notion of what 'hevenes region' would look like is preconditioned by descriptions he has read in supposed authorities on the subject [985–90].

Within *The Canterbury Tales*, it is the Wife of Bath who spotlights the element of problematic subjectivity infiltrating all writing. Commenting on an anti-feminist book treasured by her fifth husband, she declares that no 'clerk' ever speaks favourably about women other than female saints; and she adds, cryptically, 'Who peyntede the leon, tel me who?' [*Wife of Bath's Prologue*, 688–92]. Behind her mystifying question lies an Aesopic fable, as follows:

A man and a lion were debating which of them was the stronger. The man claimed he was, and to substantiate his case, he showed the lion a picture of a man triumphing over a defeated lion. The lion retorted, 'If lions were trained in painting, then you would instead see depicted the lion's victory over the man – and I'll give you good proof concerning this.' The lion fought with the man, threw him into a pit, and said, 'Now you know which of us is stronger.'

First, let us note the amusing reverberations of this fable in the Wife's marital trials of strength. She has already styled herself stubborn as a lioness [637]. Subsequently she tells how her husband confronted her interminably with the low estimate of womankind depicted in stories transmitted exclusively by men. To deal with this subjective male propaganda, she finally resorts (like the lion) to an empirical test. She tears three pages from her husband's anti-feminist book – though these emergency tactics are a somewhat paradoxical way of disproving female shrewishness – and strikes him down into the hearth. It is a most complex re-run of the fable's climax: for, if women can be 'lionesses' men can be 'lions' too, as this one proves when he leaps up like a wild 'leoun' [794] and levels her to the floor in retaliation. Dame Alys has to retrieve emotional victory out of physical defeat by recourse to an outburst of beguiling melodramatic sentiment far beyond the wit of the fable's mere male when he was prostrate in the pit: 'hastow slayn me, false theef? . . . Er I be deed, yet wol I kisse thee' [800–2].

What are the further implications of the fable? Clearly the Wife insinuates that the male literary establishment perpetuates a 'picture' of female vice that suits the male ego. In appealing to stories of vicious women as evidence, *clerkes* argue their opponents' inferiority on the basis of narrative models subjectively fashioned by men, and often, in the Wife's jocular view, fashioned by men embittered through personal circumstances such as impotent old age [697–710]. If women were trained to write (if these lionesses could paint), the boot she says would be on the other foot and the 'wikkednesse' of men would be anatomised in a million volumes [693–6]. However, a moment's reflection shows us that this would not result in breaking out of the subjective syndrome she has exposed, because her inspiring idea of a massive feminist literary counter-attack would simply oppose one partisan abuse of story with another. Chaucer has disconcertingly suggested that all art – all narrative – is distorted by the self-oriented perceptions of the artist, without offering here any solution to this predicament.

It was a predicament he would have noticed when he translated Boethius's philosophical treatise. The point is there made that no human has fully objective knowledge of the world: something we 'know' is understood by us not in terms of the independent nature of that something, but only subjectively in terms of our individual capacity for understanding it [Boethius V, prose 4]. Consequently, when Virgil, Ovid or Chaucer writes about Dido and seeks to 'know' her story, or when *clerkes* seek to project 'truth' about women, they cannot be passive transmitters of independent received wisdom or *auctoritee*. Chaucer has already made the 'modern' discovery, 'that an observer is inescapably part of what he observes, that no simple distinction can be made between subject and object, perceiver and perceived' (Kolve 1984, p.218). That discovery explains his reluctance to assume the medieval role of an *Auctor* relaying hypothetically authoritative stories with authoritative morals. He knew that personal hang-ups sabotage an individual's objective response to stories and condition an individual's retelling of them (Spearing 1983, pp. 196–9).

How, then, could he strip his own narratives of egotistical intent (*entente*)? Prior to the *Tales*, he tried out a kind of authorial disappearing-act. His stories told themselves in the voice of a seemingly humble, earnest and innocent narrator. The general effect is to cajole us into active participation, since we find ourselves shouldering the responsibility of constructing meanings which elude the amiable and easily impressed narrator. Except in the *General Prologue*, the *Tales* supersede that strategy by hiding Chaucer's authorial activity behind more robustly 'independent' storytellers – Knight, Miller and so forth. This mechanism cannot cancel the fact of his authorship, but it does enable him to confront the problem of literary subjectivity, in three ways: (1) he exposes storytellers in the act of using narrative for private ends (e.g. the Reeve's story enacts a private vendetta against the Miller); (2) he *capitalises* on human subjectivity, making us respect the vitality of those differing viewpoints which prompt a miller to present one kind of tale and a prioress another; and (3) in so doing he challenges us to reckon with our own subjectivity as readers.

The spectres of authorial *entente* and of dubious 'authority' haunt the *Tales* in all sorts of ways. The Nun's Priest, for example, seems to burlesque conventions of narrative edification. He deduces from his story platitudes on vanity and discretion which do not add up to most readers' total sense of the tale's significance. If the tale carries collective wisdom, it is a wisdom too rich and subtle to be reduced to tidy formulae of morality. By contrast in the case of the Pardoner, we have the spectacle of a clear-cut morally efficacious narrative against greed, which however its author says he normally uses with an 'yvel entencioun' [*Pardoner's Prologue*, 408], to line his own pockets. On the one hand this suggests that a story's inherent moral strength can actually exist independently of whatever egotism its teller may suffer from. But, on the other hand, since the Host repudiates this hypocrite in a devastating onslaught, it does not appear that Chaucer will allow the fallibility of an author *not* to become a crucial issue.

We may well wonder about Chaucer's own position. The design of the *Tales* permits him to indulge his talent for comic, though not always mild, satire without technically being responsible for it. We experience the satire as an inevitable expression of animosities – the pilgrims are needling each other. Yet we know Chaucer really did the writing, and it is tempting to conjecture that he pointed a wry finger at his precarious authorial perch in the curious performance of the Manciple, probably envisaged as the last tale before the Parson shuts up the storytelling.

The *Manciple's Tale* concerns Phoebus, i.e. Apollo, represented as a medieval gentleman and as a sort of arch-poet expert in song and minstrelsy. He has taught his pet white crow to 'countrefete the speche of every man . . . whan he sholde telle a tale' [134–5]; the crow therefore sounds very like the pilgrim Chaucer who purports to repeat all the pilgrims' tales word for word. Soon, Phoebus's wife commits adultery, and the crow, which has seen all, uses its power of speech to inform its master that he has been cuckolded. The information is true: it is also driven home in a distinctly satirical manner.

In great fury, Phoebus murders his wife, then 'breaks his

minstrelsy' [267], smashes up harp and lute. But later, full of remorse, he condemns the crow on second thoughts as a treacherous witness who has deceived him with a 'false tale' [293]. Phoebus's attitude to that 'tale' is now distorted by a surge of personal affection for his dead wife, so he punishes the crow, turning it black and depriving it of song (thus silencing the tale-imitating powers of his disciple). The crow will henceforth become an authoritative edifying example of 'treachery justly avenged'.

The Manciple concludes with a long-winded and in a sense paltry moral: remember the crow, restrain your speech, don't let your tongue give offence. All the same, this little Ovidian parable perhaps communicates a poet's genuine anxieties – for example, the anxiety that, whatever his desire to make stories represent 'truth', his satirical truths will not strike some readers as either funny or true, and will be irretrievably liable to perverse misunderstanding. The crow is a storyteller who cannot control interpretation of his tale. A poet who wants to eliminate these risks of authorship can easily do so. It is just a matter of 'breaking his minstrelsy', depriving his various voices of their tongues, and ceasing to write at all.

Questions of intent

We might expect Chaucer's sensitivity on the subject of authorial intention to be complemented by a fertile interest in the whole question of human intention. The tales do not disappoint us in this respect. To read them is to become freshly conscious how spoken words and actions constitute the public display of an individual's *entente*. Few other poets have so deftly explored that process of display, or have so triumphantly mimicked the excessive sincerity projected by an insincere speaker. On occasion, also, Chaucer creates speech which presents someone in the very act of deluding himself about his motives: a good example is January's declaration of his *entente* to marry [*Merchant's Tale*, 1396–468], chronically confusing prudence and piety with an elderly lecher's noxious desire to possess soft female flesh within the sanctifying institution of matrimony.

There was in any case a heightened awareness of the importance of intention in Chaucer's period, for reasons that are hinted at in the *Wife of Bath's Prologue*. At one point she mentions her 'gossib' (best friend), to whom she confided her own, and her husband's, every private thought or act; she would communicate even such glorious minutiae as the fact that her husband had pissed on a wall [529–42]. Consequently this 'gossib', says the Wife, 'knew myn herte, and eek my privetee [secrets], / Bet than oure parisshe preest, so moot I thee!' [531–2]. To understand this passing jest, we need to note how intensively the Church concentrated on the sacrament of Confession in the later Middle Ages, exhorting the individual to confess every culpable deed, word, or intention to a priest at regular intervals. Effective absolution depended on a person's heartfelt contrition. Chaucer's Parson tells us that contrition 'hideth . . . in the herte of hym that is verray repentaunt, right as the roote of a tree hydeth hym in the erthe' [*Parson's Tale*, 112]. Thus, although a priest might be mildly indifferent to the urination habits of your spouse, he was decidedly interested in your *herte* and your *privetee* – especially those queasy hidden motives which determined the state of your soul.

One cardinal principle of confessional teaching reflected in Chaucer's work is that unrepentant evil intent makes a person's heart vulnerable to the Devil's most powerful temptations. A copybook example occurs in the *Pardoner's Tale* when the youngest of three layabouts who have discovered a heap of gold is on his way to fetch provisions, revolving in his *herte* the attraction of somehow appropriating the entire windfall to himself. The man's frame of mind gives the Devil the right to 'putte in his thoghte' the idea of poisoning his companions (so bringing himself to perdition), because it is his 'fulle entente' to eliminate them 'and nevere to repente' [837–50]. Just how this doctrine ricochets upon the Pardoner himself, who gloats that his 'entente' is entirely directed towards personal gain [*Pardoner's Prologue*, 403], is left to us to work out.

Another unreformable character bent on profiteering is the Summoner in the *Friar's Tale*. At the very moment when it is established that he has no intention to repent his extortionate practices, he is whisked off to hell by the Devil in person [1618–36]. And, so that we shall not underestimate the significance of interior motivation at this climax, the tale incorporates earlier a contrasting episode concerning a carter who consigns his horses to the 'feend' because they cannot pull his cart out of the mud. Observing this, the Summoner naïvely encourages his Devil companion to grab what is apparently being offered him on a plate, but the Devil knows the carter's *entente* belies his words – as it transpires when the cart begins to move and its owner now showers blessings upon his horses [1537–65].

The Devil sums up: 'The carl spak oo thing, but he thoghte another' [1568]. Although this might mean that the blessings correspond to the man's thoughts more closely than the preceding curses, I think most readers would interpret curses and blessings alike as casually exaggerated expressions of emotion: first frustration, then relief. In neither case did what he 'spak' literally articulate his 'thoghte'. And that is precisely the sort of gap which Chaucer, specialist in irony, cultivates in many of his tales.

What Chaucer envisages as the normative ideal, against which deviations are to be measured, is a total accord between the private thought and its public projection. Virginia, in the *Physician's Tale,* manifests this harmony (though in a specifically 'wommanly' manner [43–57]. Not only is she a paragon of disciplined inner virtue, but also her style of speech is disciplined and 'pleyn'; it is morally resonant, it is proper to her station in life, and she uses no 'countrefeted termes' to 'seme wys' (i.e. her language shows no bogus pretentiousness). In short she is a model of exterior-interior integrity. So too is Griselda in the *Clerk's Tale.* Whatever sufferings her husband Walter inflicts upon her, she declares that never 'in word or werk' will she regret that she has given him her 'herte in hool entente' [858–61]. Walter watches her closely to see whether 'by word or contenance' she will reveal rebellious motives, but finds in her a constant harmony of 'herte and . . . visage' [708–11].

Paradoxically, Walter's determination to test whether Griselda's protestations genuinely express an inner commitment to obedience involves him in contrasting duplicity. Her dedicated *entente* delights his *herte,* yet to carry through his tests he keeps up a front of 'drery contenance' [671–2]. Only a residual sense of his long-term benevolence allows us to distinguish his fraudulence from that of the Wife of Bath, who put on a widow-like show of 'sory cheere' at the funeral of husband number four – but in truth 'wepte but smal' because the shapely legs of prospective number five were before her eyes in the cortege [*Wife of Bath's Prologue*, 586–99]. Not that the Wife's 'hypocrisy' warrants simple moral condemnation, either: she flouts funeral taboos with audaciously disarming cheek, and, besides, her fourth husband had been promiscuous. In her world, where lion eats lion, no innocents are conspicuously harmed by her counterfeit intent.

That, of course, is the sticking-point for Chaucer. To practise deceit upon an innocence such as Virginia's is a 'sovereyn pestilence' [*Physician's Tale*, 91]. The converse of Virginia's integrity is perhaps most elaborately presented in another context, the *Squire's Tale*, where a falcon operatically bewails her deception by a male bird who courted her. On the surface he was all lavish attention and 'humble cheere', projecting a hue of sincerity which covered his shabby *entente*. She gave him her love because he proffered such ravishing expressions of devotion, so 'painting' his words and behaviour that she assumed a corresponding truth lay in his heart. The result, for her, was utter emotional desolation, though the storyteller inflates this to the verge of spoof. After a while her partner had to fly away (on chivalric business, as it were), and immediately revealed his 'doubleness' by taking up with an inferior kite instead [504–629]. Small wonder that the Squire imagines elsewhere in his tale a magic mirror – portable lie-detector – in which you can see 'openly' a man's ulterior intentions towards you [132–41].

Counterfeit *entente* is a major common denominator in the *Tales*. To match the falcon's spurious lover (who was, we were also told, a serpent lurking beneath flowers until the moment came to 'byte'), there is the Pardoner, who spits venom at his opponents 'under hewe / of hoolynesse' [*Pardoner's Prologue*, 421–2]; and there is a vicious sultaness, 'serpent under femynynytee', who receives her son's bride with motherly 'glad cheere' while coolly planning a bloody massacre at the wedding-feast [*Man of Law's Tale*, 358f.]. We may again compare the bird lover's protestations with those of the fox in the *Nun's Priest's Tale*, disclaiming any intention of 'harm or vileynye' as he manoeuvres to trap the cockerel [3286–7].

The ironist in Chaucer often makes him linger captivatingly over the blandishments of these dealers in 'painted' sincerity. We listen with apprehensive awe to an expertly hypocritical alchemist (in the *Canon's Yeoman's Tale*) who ingratiatingly cultivates a priest's trust by promptly returning some cash he has borrowed from him and taking that opportunity to advertise his reliability: ' nevere falshede in myn herte I mente' [1044–51]. But in the heart of the alchemist there lurk the Devil's own thoughts, aimed at corrupting the innocent priest with avarice, so that he will take the bait of a useless recipe for gold-making powder which can be his for a princely sum.

The alchemist's tricks are narrated by the Yeoman in a spirit of highly charged moral indignation. The Yeoman is consumed by, and occasionally defensive about, his own bitterly hostile *entente* towards fraudulent practitioners of futile alchemical experiments, in which he has himself served a pointless apprenticeship. His embittered motivation might easily detain us, but I should like to turn instead to a wider question: how is it that frauds which are theoretically almost as repugnant as the alchemist's can in other tales become a basis for mirth, evading moral interpretation?

The *Merchant's Tale*, for instance, develops a rhetoric of moral castigation reminiscent of the Yeoman's. The Yeoman rang the rhetorical alarm bells when the priest was about to be duped by the alchemist: 'O sely [innocent] preest! . . . No thyng ne artow war of the deceite / Which that this fox yshapen hath to thee!' [1076–80]. At an equivalent point in his story, the Merchant protests against the imminent deception of January by his own squire, Damyan: 'O Januarie, dronken in plesaunce / In mariage, se how thy Damyan . . . Entendeth for to do thee vileynye' [1788–91]. But let us follow this 'vileynye' through, and assess what complicates our response to it.

Damyan has become besotted with January's young bride, May, and falls ill with longing. January, gratified by bouts of newly-wed sexual exercise, is full of solicitude for his favourite squire and trustingly sends May to comfort Damyan. Subsequently she reads the youth's love-letter, and disposes of it, in the toilet: an unromantic event, next to which the poem's rhetoric seems incongruous. It proves difficult for squire and lady to consummate their desires as they forthwith intend, because her old husband suddenly goes blind and becomes formidably possessive.

A duplicate key to January's private garden is the solution. Damyan, who by now knows May's every *entente* better than her husband, lets himself into the garden. January is nearby with May, mingling professions of his devotion with thinly veiled bribery: through loyalty to him she'll earn all his property. Her response is to avow her regard for her soul, for her honour, and for the tender flower of her wifehood, cursing herself if she should ever dream of infidelity. In the next second, nonchalantly two-faced, she signals to Damyan that he should climb a tree [2152–211].

At this stage there is an extraordinary interruption in the narrative. Pluto (King of the Otherworld) and his consort Proserpina are introduced – they represent a sort of updated antique Chorus commenting on the action. Pluto has had enough of the old routine of female treachery which May is about to perpetuate, and proposes to return January's sight when she commits her *vileynye*. Proserpina, Counsel for Women's Defence, retorts that, if so, she will equip May, 'and alle wommen after, for hir sake', with some bold answer to extricate herself from such an eventuality [2237–319].

When, therefore, the tender wife cajoles her husband into allowing her to climb Damyan's tree in order to satisfy her yearning for 'pears', January's eyes are opened to the sight of her ensuing convulsive copulation. And, as predicted, May has a magnificently bold answer to squash January's outrage. On peril of her soul she has, following sound medical advice, discovered that there is no better cure for her husband's blindness than for her to 'strugle with a man upon a tree'. God knows, she exclaims, she *'dide it in ful good entente'* [2371–5].

Viperous hypocrisy, indeed: but we are not inclined to cry out against gross moral turpitude. The reasons for this are quite complex. They include the fact that January ('dronken in plesaunce') is of course no innocent corroded by the poisonous *entente* of his deceivers. His soul is riddled with conceit and lust already; moreover, his intolerable possessiveness seems well revenged through May's resort to alternative solace. Then, there is the sheer hilarity of sex-in-a-tree (requiring, one would think, stunning gymnastic co-ordination to make it anything *other* than a desperate 'strugle').

There is however yet another consideration, which derives from Chaucer's exploitation of the Pluto–Proserpina chorus. What they do, in effect, is to *generalise* the tale's deception in such a way that we are obliged to perceive January *versus* May as a contest of wits played out according to the conventions of an ancient game. Let us call the game 'Spying Husbands, Agile Youths, and Wily Wives'. Wily Wives (coached by Proserpina) are always top seeds, and they usually win the tie-breaks. The attraction of the game is to watch their deft footwork at the net. Chaucer quells moral reflection on May by concentrating our minds on the art of that game.

This does not mean that moral implications evaporate altogether. We recall the proverb, 'Many a truth is spoken in jest', and if May converts January's earnestness into a *jape* (to borrow a Chaucerian expression), there is a residual taste of earnest left in the jape. In my view that taste enriches the sauce in all Chaucer's 'sauciest' tales. It is true that he sometimes speaks as though *ernest* and *game* exist in separate watertight compartments. But in practice he is clearly interested in overlapping them.

One species of overlap appears in the Host, who is fond of addressing home truths to the pilgrims under colour of jest. For example, having cast aspersions on the Cook's reheated pies and fly-ridden shop, he urges him not to take umbrage, for 'A man may seye ful sooth in game and pley' [*Cook's Prologue*, 4355]. The Cook is not much amused. He retorts that a true jest is a sour jest and threatens a retaliatory satire on innkeepers. The Host has perhaps steered too close to that variety of 'double tonge' whereby people affect to speak 'in game and pley, and yet they speke of wikked entente' [*Parson's Tale*, 643].

Two other instances of playful intention merit attention. Each in its own way connects *pley* (not unnaturally) with risk. One occurs when the Wife of Bath prepares to report how she bulldozed her way through the combined forces of husbands and anti-feminist doctrine. We are not to be upset by what she says, because her 'entente is nat but for to pleye' [*Wife of Bath's Prologue*, 189–92]. This performs several functions: (a) it proclaims her zestful transformation of life into a game; (b) it allows for an elusive, creative interaction between 'fact' and playful exaggeration in her reminiscences; and (c) it is an escape-clause for the poet, lest the Establishment should pillory him for letting sensuality loose, to the corruption of tender readers.

The second example arises in the *Franklin's Tale*. Squire Aurelius, whose amorous *entente* has never yet dawned on the happily wed Dorigen, nerves himself to tell her of his passion. Dorigen first responds with a decisive rebuff: but, 'after that, in pley' she adds that her affections are obtainable if he can cause the coastal rocks nearby to disappear [980–98]. Once again we have a demonstration of Chaucer's concern with intention in speech. Dorigen has only just grasped what Aurelius 'mente' by numerous previous attempts to catch her eye. At this very juncture, she muddies her own *entente* with a 'playful' promise, only too easily misconstrued into earnest. The result is near-disaster.

Chaucer's most capacious review of the mystery of human intention and its unpredictable consequences is reserved for the *Knight's Tale*. Here the subject is put into panoramic perspective, a perspective which perhaps shadows, too, most of the examples we have mentioned. The heartfelt sincerity of the tale's protagonists is not in doubt; if anything, their *entente* is so hugely soulful as to invite a wry smile. The emphasis, this time, is upon *thwarted* intention, which furnishes an incessant rhythm in the narrative. For instance, Palamon escapes from Theseus's prison and pauses in a nearby grove, planning to go by night to his home in Thebes, raise an army, make war on Theseus, and win the hand of Emelye or die: that is the sum of his 'entente' [1487]. It is thwarted because next morning his rival Arcite appears in the grove. So they agree on an intention to fight each other to the death tomorrow. On the morrow that intention is thwarted in turn by the intervention of Theseus; and so on.

Persistently frustrated intention breeds cynicism, which is intermittently voiced in the *Knight's Tale*. It is left to Theseus, at the end, to affirm providential 'ordinaunce' nevertheless [3012], and to argue that the creating mind which set the world in motion designed all with 'heigh entente', knowing full well 'what thereof he mente' [2987–90]. The difficulty of understanding that cosmic intent is, one might observe, paralleled everywhere in the *Canterbury Tales* by the difficulty of penetrating (without a magic mirror) the motives governing one person's behaviour towards another.

Chaucer may finally be said to express a double impulse himself on this matter. On the one hand, he implies that eternal vigilance against deception is necessary. But on the other he implies that, since one individual's objectives regularly cancel out another's, sanity is only preserved by constructive patience, on the assumption that all would be seen to cohere for the best if we could but fathom the supernal *entente*.

Narrative resonance

In the Introduction to this 'Appraisal' I spoke of a 'play of mind' in *The Canterbury Tales*. A major factor in that play of mind is something that might variously be termed 'allusiveness', 'width of reference', 'layered texture' and so forth; a technique enabling Chaucer to orchestrate narrative with harmonies and discords so as to build imaginatively vibrant structures from the simplest of inherited stories.

The term used here to describe the technique will be *resonance*. Without any intention of campaigning to found a critical School of Resonance, I shall first suggest that the word is not unsuited to Chaucer's poetry, if we consider the definition: 'reinforcement or prolongation of sound by synchronous vibration'.

For Chaucer, sound constitutes a 'reverberacioun' of air [*Summoner's Tale*, 2233–5]. Writing in a playfully scientific vein, he is inclined to insist that 'every speche that ys spoken' is merely a form of broken air, and even, it seems, inclined to think of poets as people who noisily trumpet the windy reputations of their heroes and heroines [*House of Fame*, 765–81, 1624ff.]. But these are the more sportive reflections of what was in him, as we saw in the section 'Social and political historicism', a strong interest in the spoken, oral dimension of his art. The fiction of 'live' storytelling in the *Tales* allows him to develop this interest.

One speaker self-conscious about his sound-effects is the Pardoner, who says he customarily rings out his pulpit rhetoric 'as round as gooth a belle' [*Pardoner's Prologue*, 329–31]. However, the emphasis on sound occurs also in less predictable contexts than that. We are told in the *General Prologue* for example that the Merchant conversed most solemnly, 'Sownynge alwey th'encrees of his wynnyng' [274–5 (probably meaning: 'continually proclaiming the increase in his profits')]. Both here and in the case of the Clerk, whose speech by contrast was 'Sownynge in moral vertu' [307], *sownynge* may technically mean 'according (with)' or 'tending (towards)'; but I doubt whether that excludes an implication that the Merchant 'sounded off' about his financial coups and that the Clerk's talk was resoundingly wholesome.

Although one could go on from here to consider how a tale such as the Prioress's differs orally from, say, the Shipman's, we shall concentrate instead on more fundamental techniques of resonance in the poetry. For instance, wordplay immediately comes to mind as a means of attaining 'synchronous vibration' of meaning, and the modern discovery of Chaucer's interest in wordplay has culminated in a whole dictionary of his bawdier puns (Ross 1972). The tales frequently project a punster-poet's delight in equivocation. Thus in the *Pardoner's Tale*, when the youngest of the three 'riotoures' plans to dispose of his two fellows, the reason he gives at the apothecary's shop for buying poison is that he wants to kill 'his rattes', a polecat, and every other vermin on his property [851–8]. This pretext vibrates in our reading, not only because it mimics a liar's tendency to over-enforce his lies but also because his comrades seem indeed no better than vermin, plotting to murder *him* on his return.

Verbal repetition might be deemed another means of making a word 'vibrate' in our minds. This is surely the case with the word *brother* and its associates *cosyn* and *felawe* in the *Knight's Tale*.

The tale's two Theban youths Palamon and Arcite, captured together by Theseus, are cousins. They have also sworn a sentimental mutual brotherhood, as Palamon reproachfully reminds Arcite ('my leeve [dear] brother') when Arcite presumes to fall in love with Emelye moments after he himself has [1136; also 1131, 1147]. The nub of Arcite's retort, slotted between increasingly empty expressions of endearment – 'my brother', 'leeve brother' – is that where love is concerned it's 'Ech man for hymself' [1181–4].

The Knight stresses the pathos of their rancorous brotherhood at numerous points. For example, when they prepare to fight to death over their jealousy, each helps to arm the other 'As freendly as he were his owene brother' [1651–2]. Again, after a fatal accident ruins Arcite's prospect of marrying Emelye, he commends Palamon 'his cosyn deere' to her as a 'worthy' suitor in a belated spirit of generosity which – since he is dying anyway – he can by now well afford [2762–97].

The collision between the competitive instincts of passionate love and the wider principle of humane fellowship attains its greatest resonance at two rather different junctures in the tale. One, just before the rival lovers' private combat, takes the form of an outburst by the narrator: 'O Cupide, out of alle charitee! / O regne, that wolt no felawe have with thee!' [1623–4]. That is to say, one kind of love (Cupid-governed, with a possible pun on 'cupidity') overrules another (Christian charity towards fellow beings). The poignant rhetoric here sets up biblical reverberations, invoking texts such as 'though I have all faith, so that I could remove mountains, and have not charity, I am nothing' (I Corinthians 13:2). There is in addition a teasing link back to the Wife of Bath in the *General Prologue*, who became 'out of alle charitee' if any wife dared to take precedence over her at church [449–52]. There are other considerations in her case, but it can be seen that 'out of alle charitee' introduces a kind of religious double-bass into these passages.

The other moment at which brotherhood is notably orchestrated in the *Knight's Tale* occurs soon after Arcite's every-man-for-himself declaration. Theseus is visited by his friend Perotheus, and the Knight offers a brief aside to the effect that there was such a bond of affection between these two 'That whan that oon was deed, soothly to telle, / His felawe wente and soughte hym doun in helle' [1196–1201]. It is an oddly bland and offhand way of mentioning a comradely, epical rescue from hell. One reason for the brusqueness is the possibility that this much (borrowed from *The Romance of the Rose*) was all Chaucer knew of the legend. In any case, his passing nod is well calculated momentarily to recall heroic displays of manly *felaweshipe* in the 'olde bookes' and even to hint – on the outer fringes of its reverberation – at Christ's own selfless rescue of humankind from hell. The Knight judiciously skips ahead with his narrative, lest the impact of this potentially far-reaching implied comment on the unbrotherly Palamon and Arcite should too decisively undermine our sympathy for them.

Very many of the tales play absorbingly on religious topics. It seems we lack critical terminology to describe the intermittent 'stereo' effect this produces. 'Allegory' is inaccurate (we are not talking of continuous double meaning); 'parody' is too narrowly nuanced; and 'allusion' too lame. That is why I am resorting to 'resonance', which perhaps better expresses the enhancement of significance created through an adroit echo, such as we find at the climax of the *Friar's Tale*. There, as we saw in the last section, an unrepentant extortioner is seized by the Devil, who declares, 'Thou shalt with me to helle yet to-nyght' [1636]. In a flash, the tale cross-connects with biblical narrative. For, of the two thieves crucified next to Christ, one was inspired with penitence and made a last-minute appeal, to which Christ responded 'Verily I say unto thee, Today shalt thou be with me in paradise' (Luke 23:39–43; noted by Huppé 1964, p.200). Since the tale's rapacious summoner ('this false theef' [1338]) has spurned his own eleventh-hour chance to repent, Chaucer's reversal of Christ's words chimes in here with devastating effect, aligning the summoner with the second, hardened thief at the crucifixion.

We might put things another way and say that Chaucer has a strategic eye for opportunities to collide his narratives with religious materials. This happens again in the *Pardoner's Tale*, whose three villains (a sort of Unholy Trinity) undertake a drunken quest to slay Death [699, 710]. As Bishop suggests, their quest amounts to a 'blasphemously materialistic application of St Paul's promise that "Death shall be swallowed up in victory"' (in Anderson, *Casebook*, p.220).

In a different key the Pardoner betrays his own materialistic imperviousness to the doctrines he mouths, through a simple countryside image. He colourfully describes how he gesticulates in the pulpit, jerking his head to and fro like 'a dowve sittynge on a berne' [*Pardoner's Prologue*, 395–7]. I agree with the supposition that Chaucer means us to sense here a degradation of that gift of fervent eloquence which derived from the Holy Spirit – invariably symbolised as a *dove* in the Middle Ages. That the Pardoner blindly reduces the dove of the spirit to neck-twisting farmyard bird is imaginatively consistent with his subsequent remark about the souls of the dead: they can 'go blackberrying' for all he cares [405–6].

The dove-image can be said to contain 'optional' resonance; it seems to vibrate suggestively, but we can't prove it. In my view the tales generate innumerable subtleties of this kind, which the reader is challenged to hear. Since the *Miller's Tale* is an especially teasing instance, we shall conclude this section by sampling the bait it offers.

The tale concerns Nicholas's plot to get his landlord into a tub (makeshift dinghy) in the loft, awaiting a second Noah's Flood, so that he can meanwhile make love to the landlord's young wife. Since it was widely argued that the original Noah's Flood represented God's attempt to wipe out rampant promiscuity, there is an obvious comicality in re-running it to allow for a night of illicit sex.

There are also possible secondary resonances. For example, Nicholas bamboozles the landlord by claiming that, as an astrological expert, he has gained access to top secret celestial information about the imminent 'flood' and how to survive it. Bearing in mind that his namesake St Nicholas was legendary (a) for being picked out by a heavenly voice to become a bishop, and (b) for his miraculous ability to bring seafarers safely through storms, the narrative interaction with religious lore seems to accumulate entertainingly.

Furthermore, Nicholas has lent colour to his claim by maintaining a guru-like vigil in his room, gaping up at the stratosphere in a trance [3444–5, 3472–3]. To judge from chapter 57 of *The Cloud of Unknowing* (a medieval English handbook on the art of spiritual contemplation), this posture rather precisely caricatures that associated with the untutored or sham contemplative: i.e. one who supposes that lifting up the heart to God means literally staring at the stars, trying to pierce the firmament in search of angel-song or gaping open-mouthed in expectation of imbibing spiritual nourishment.

Finally, there are optional resonances at the tale's finale, surrounding the vengeful action of Nicholas's rival, Absolon, after the latter has been duped into kissing the heroine's arse. Absolon obtains from a nearby smithy a red-hot iron implement. He proceeds to ram it against Nicholas's own nether quarters. Remembering the medieval logic whereby the fires of hell punish the fires of lechery, it is tempting to envisage Absolon at this point as a comic stand-in for the fiend, requiting Nicholas (through a scalding quasi-homosexual attack!) for his fornication. The smith's expression 'Cristes foo!' when he lends the implement – 'Ey, Cristes foo! what wol ye do therwith?' [3782] – lends support to this idea if 'foo' is taken to mean 'foe' and taken to apply to Absolon, not just as an incidental oath.

Alternatively or simultaneously the heated ploughing implement, if not actually phallic, sounds like a wonderfully palpable version of the 'firebrand' which medieval Venus conventionally wields to fuel the heat of love [*Merchant's Tale*, 1727, 1777]. Only, its effect in the burlesque world of the *Miller's Tale* is to wreck Nicholas's sexual caper, causing him to scream for water, so triggering in his landlord's imagination the anticipated flood, and thence indeed terminating further promiscuity.

These readings take up what seem to me to be some of the more sophisticated resonances in the *Miller's Tale*. I may have strained too hard, like the gaping mystic, to detect them, though they are not lacking in textual foundation. Some of them approximate to suggestions by other critics, some not. At all events we have glimpsed in this section an important aspect of that *heigh wit* which the tales display, and which confirms that we need what I earlier called (in the Introduction to this 'Appraisal') a mentally agile 'Jankyn approach' if we are to relish the vibrant play of significance in Chaucer's poetry.

An audacious art

It has been stated by one editor that Chaucer's poem *Troilus and Criseyde*, in comparison with its source, displays an increased 'energy' and 'vehemence'. Chaucer introduces greater 'onslaughts of feeling'; the general effect is 'as if a stronger light is thrown over the original and a more deeply etched picture emerges' (Windeatt 1984, pp. 5–7). These remarks point to a quality of vivid intensity which I believe to be equally characteristic of *The Canterbury Tales*, and which was probably what Beaumont responded to in the sixteenth century when he praised Chaucer's power 'to possesse his Readers with a stronger imagination of seeing that done before their eyes, which they reade, than any other that euer writ' (Kolve 1984, p.19).

There is evidence that Chaucer would have been particularly gratified by the nature of this tribute. A scientific commentary on sound in one of his poems (mentioned in the previous section) is offered by a speaking eagle who takes pride in communicating difficult ideas in words so 'palpable' that one may shake them by the beak [*House of Fame*, 865–9]. Although this eagle is a burlesque figure, it is reasonable to infer that his relish for 'palpability' of language reflects the poet's own aspirations too.

No doubt Chaucer's palpability sometimes strikes us as a matter of specific detail: those rats and that capon-killing polecat, for instance, referred to by the villain in the *Pardoner's Tale*. But we shall consider something else which excites our strong imagination of seeing what we read done before our eyes, and that is the streak of audacious exaggeration which intensifies so much of the speech, emotion and action in the *Tales*. Isolating just two aspects of this intensification, we shall look first at 'exhibitionism' within the work, and secondly at elaborations of *fantasie* (especially as they contribute to the poet's presentation of love).

In the *General Prologue* we find the pilgrim Chaucer applying for a licence to introduce all manner of audacities, under pretext that, if he is to record the speech and behaviour of the pilgrims accurately (never mind that his *alter ego* is composing them), he must reproduce even their broadest language: for, 'Whoso shal telle a tale after a man, . . . He may nat spare, although he were his brother' [731–7]. This licence for 'not sparing' (not holding back) is tantamount to a *carte blanche* for Chaucer's storytellers to express themselves with colourful and provocative intensity. It is tantamount to an ingenious excuse for suspending literary decorum and allowing speakers to let rip, exhibiting either themselves or those they scorn as daringly as the poet wishes.

I suppose the two most virtuoso exhibitions are those of the Pardoner and the Wife of Bath. In neither case is any obvious motive offered for their unrestrained self-display, which relates to – yet seems not simply reducible to – a medieval literary device of frank confession or self-exposure by a personification of sin. Each seems constructed to court audience shock or outrage, as if out of some compulsive bravado. Thus the Pardoner brazenly exhibits such extravagances as his vicious determination to extract money or provisions from the poorest widow even if her children should consequently die of hunger [*Pardoner's Prologue*, 448–51].

The Wife's brash disclosures arise, she claims, out of an 'entente . . . to pleye' and out of her 'fantasye' (here probably 'whim' or 'fancy', but it is a suggestive word as we shall see [*Wife of Bath's Prologue*, 189–92]). However, she is also egged on, interestingly enough, by her fellow-exhibitionist the Pardoner, who after interrupting prods her, 'Telle forth youre tale, spareth for no man' [186]. She hardly needs his encouragement. Arch-scourge of men, she revels in her shrill account of the incessant scolding by which she subjugated her first three husbands. She 'wolde nat spare hem' (restrain her campaign against them), not even if the Pope himself had sat beside them at the supper-table, as she puts it with glorious hyperbole [420–1].

These examples perhaps suggest that the strategy of no-holds-barred audacity yields effects which are lifelike precisely because they are larger than life. They manifest the sharp-etched quality of a cartoon, whether entertainingly (the Wife) or disturbingly (the Pardoner). 'Not-sparing' implies that the normally unsayable will get said with vivid candour, as indeed happens in the best cartoons. Chaucer presses as it were a 'release' button in such cases, triggering his most colourfully mischievous or satirical creativity.

A sense of how he feels able to cut loose in this way emerges at the end of the *Canon's Yeoman's Prologue*. The alchemist Canon, discovering that the Yeoman (prompted by the Host) is beginning to divulge the secrets of his dubious craft, beats a hasty retreat. This frees the Yeoman to pour out his pent-up anger against the Canon and his kind without restraint. 'A!' he exclaims, '*heere shal arise game; . . .* Syn that my lord is goon, I wol nat spare' [703–18]. With the Canon's departure, Chaucer uninhibits the storyteller so that everyone can enjoy the spectacle (*game*) of searing exposure.

Just how important this release-mechanism was for Chaucer is clear from the fact that he also operates it in the Friar *versus* Summoner episode. This time the opponent is not spared even in his own presence. Hostilities commence after the *Wife of Bath's Prologue*. At first the Host struggles to preserve companionship, crying 'Pees!' to quell the animosity between the two men. But, seeing that their mutual sniping continues so virulent that it threatens to impede the Friar's anti-Summoner story, he abandons peacemaking tactics in a now familiar way: 'Ne spareth nat', he advises the Friar [*Friar's Tale*, 1335–6]. The pattern repeats itself when the Host enjoins the Summoner not to 'spare' his rival in telling of a hypocritical friar.

Now, although we can enjoy this *game* of intensified satiric exposure in the knowledge that it is conducted by unstoppably malicious combatants, their unsparing aggression still contravenes the stated interests of group *pees*. Moreover it is disturbing to perceive that 'not-sparing', translated into action within the *Friar's Tale*, assumes sinister proportions when it takes the form of unmitigated extortion from human prey [1435–8]. It seems that Chaucer does not take out his licence for freebooting satire without acknowledging the cost, in terms of the potential damage to ideals of socially and morally desirable self-restraint.

Self-restraint is also endangered by *fantasie*, whose presence in the *Tales* we are now to consider. *Fantasie* has a slightly more technical sense for Chaucer than its modern equivalent. It denotes the domination of a person's thought by often delusive (but not necessarily 'fantastic') images or ideas; a sort of mental obsession indulged to the detriment of objectivity. Chaucer keenly develops narrative opportunities for exploring *fantasie*, since this is another means of heightening his poetry and taking us to the more spectacular extremities of human behaviour.

The *Franklin's Tale* provides a classic example. Its heroine, Dorigen, is stricken by her husband's absence into a grief so intense that it threatens to 'slay' her heart [840]. Eventually her friends' patient arguments begin to 'print' rational consolation upon her emotional misery [832–4]; but their plan to dispel 'hire derke fantasye' [844] with seaside recreation misfires, since she then starts forlornly surveying the ocean for some ship that might bring back her husband, and grows faint with terror as she muses over the menacing rocks that imperil his return. Clearly these rocks loom large in her obsessive *fantasie*, with the result that her consuming desire for them to sink becomes the condition upon which she cryptically half-offers her love to her suitor Aurelius.

In my view Chaucer projects Dorigen's state of mind up to this point with characteristically judicious sympathy. He indicates that her self-lacerating concentration on Arveragus's absence amounts to a 'rage' (extravagant emotion [836]), straining the tolerance of her kindly friends. But at the same time he invests positively in her the pathos of the human capacity for feeling. If a hyper-active impressionable imagination like hers engenders futile distress, that does not entirely discredit the capacity for feeling which is associated with such impressionability.

I believe this point is unexpectedly confirmed in the *Miller's*

Tale, where Chaucer embroiders trickster Nicholas's forecast of a flood with such winning detail that his rugged landlord, John, is overwhelmed with anguish: hallucinatory images of waves enveloping his 'hony' Alisoun crowd his mind [3614–17]. She is of course by no means *his* honey, and his fear of this implausible flood is put into perspective as a crazy *fantasie* at the tale's end [3835, 3840]. Nevertheless, his susceptibility to emotive images prompts Chaucer to risk, against the grain of this joy-riding tale, a touch of solemnity which momentarily dignifies John's mental fancies. They are the stuff of which emotions no less piercing than Dorigen's might be made:

> Lo, which a greet thyng is affecioun! [emotion]
> Men may dyen of ymaginacioun
> So depe may impressioun be take. [3611–13]

The chief exemplars of absorbed reverie are, naturally enough, the various courtly suitors in the tales. Chaucer sustains the medieval literary convention that a male lover, once smitten with the 'arrows' of beauty, nurses an all-consuming image of the beloved in an agony of secretive fear and frustration. According to the *Knight's Tale*, in acute cases this locked-in obsession produces a mental malfunction as serious as the 'mania' caused when fluids of Melancholy invade the imaginative portion of the brain (the 'celle fantastik' [1372–6]). Here we have a poker-faced clinical diagnosis, one of the gambits by which Chaucer, even while committing much poetic energy to love's subjective pathos, sustains our objectivity towards it. Other gambits, both of which feature in the *Knight's Tale*, are to modulate from lyricism into wholesome mockery of the lover's eccentric moodiness – up one minute and down the next like a bucket in a well [1528–33]; and to operate equivocally on the very limits of acceptable hyperbole when expressing the lover's languishings, tears, swoons, and his lurid talk of death.

For Chaucer, then, the courtly lover is an inevitable focus of extravagance. Possessed by ungovernable emotions, the lover will commit actions which are 'heigh folye' by the standards of mature rational consideration [1798]. Thus Arcite risks his neck in returning from the safety of Thebes to Athens (where he is outlawed), but declares 'for the drede of deeth shal I nat spare / To se my lady' [1395-7 (i.e. not refrain from seeing her)]. We realise that there is an 'unsparing' dimension in love, too. Aurelius demonstrates it again in the *Franklin's Tale*. He would give the whole world, let alone the gigantic sum that an Orleans magician demands, to win Dorigen [1226-9]. And, if Dorigen in her *fantasie* suffers a 'rage' of grief, Aurelius matches her, after hearing her verdict on his love-plea, with an intensity of self-torturing sorrow that reduces him to near-insane 'ravying' [1026-7] and thence to a two-year trance 'in langour and in torment furyus' [1101-2].

Aurelius is in hysteria and can choose for himself, as the narrator mischievously remarks, 'wheither he wol lyve or dye' [1086]. But let us also notice how the introverted, obsessive characteristics of both Dorigen and Aurelius are pointedly contrasted with the uncluttered mind of her husband Arveragus. On returning to her, he is *not* 'ymaginatyf' as to whether anyone might have courted her [1094-7]: that is to say, he does *not* crowd his brain with unbalancing fancies. In one way this is a shortcoming. The result is that he doesn't hear about Dorigen's rash vow to Aurelius until too late. When he does hear, though, his controlled feelings and incisive thought as a man who restrains debilitating excesses of the imagination come as a relief to us despite the traumatic context (sending his own wife to keep an adulterous promise).

In Arveragus's self-control, we glimpse the opposite of those impulses towards excess which, I have argued, are leading strands in the audacious art of the *Tales*. The antithesis of *fantasie* is rationally controlled thought, what Chaucer calls *avysement*. (Arveragus himself is perhaps not a model of rational deliberation, for he acts too fast, though the successful outcome ensures that we retrospectively credit him with prehensile discretion.) The antithesis of 'not sparing' is, of course, 'sparing', the activity of restraining or refraining: it is a word which occurs in the *Parson's Tale* alongside fellow concepts such as temperance, moderation, and sobriety [835].

We could take up many more pages analysing self-restraint and self-control in Chaucer's poem. Paradoxically he sometimes develops them in extravagant vein, too, as in the case of Griselda in the *Clerk's Tale*. He 'etches' her hyper-controlled behaviour as daringly as he ever etches the uncontrolled mentality elsewhere.

Our conclusion must be that Chaucer explores human extravagance in triumphantly 'palpable' poetry, whose power to work upon our own imagination is enriched by the encompassing assurance that the intensities are wrought by a highly rational artist. I leave the reader to ponder therefore whether, of all the dualistic titles one might invent to express the cross-currents in this complex work, 'Excess and Restraint in *The Canterbury Tales*' would take us to the heart of the matter.

References

Critical materials cited in this book are listed below. Since they have been selected more with regard to emphatic currents in criticism than with regard to comprehensive coverage of prominent publications, a number of significant commentaries are not represented. The penultimate section of the References identifies some of these omissions. For more extensive guidance, the reader might consult (a) Rowland (1979: see 'Collections of Essays' below), or, in the case of specific tales, (b) individual volumes in the *Variorum Edition* of Chaucer's works, published by the University of Oklahoma Press under the general editorship of Paul Ruggiers, in which a survey of criticism forms part of the introduction to each tale.

My categorisation of the critics listed should be treated with circumspection, since some of them really belong in several categories at once. For that reason, the reader will sometimes find that a given critic cited in one section of the 'Survey', appears in a different section in the following bibliography. The quickest way to locate a reference is to use the Index.

Critics and Commentators

* *Names preceded by an asterisk denote the compilers of collections of essays, listed below.*

Collections of essays

Anderson, J. J., *Chaucer, 'The Canterbury Tales': A Casebook* (London, 1974).
Brewer, D. S., *Writers and their Backgrounds: Geoffrey Chaucer* (London, 1974).
　　Tradition and Innovation in Chaucer (London, 1982).
　　Chaucer: the Poet as Storyteller (London, 1984).
Donaldson, E. T., *Speaking of Chaucer* (London, 1970).

Kellogg, A. L., *Chaucer, Langland, Arthur: Essays in Middle English Literature* (New Brunswick, NJ, 1972).
Rose, D. M., *New Perspectives in Chaucer Criticism* (Norman, Okla, 1981).
Rowland, B., *Companion to Chaucer Studies*, 2nd edn (Oxford, 1979).
Wagenknecht, E., *Chaucer: Modern Essays in Criticism* (New York, 1959).

Introduction

Bloomfield, M. W., 'Contemporary Literary Theory and Chaucer' (1981, in *Rose, pp.23–36.
Eagleton, T., *Literary Theory: An Introduction* (Oxford, 1983).
Minnis, A., 'Chaucer and Comparative Literary Theory' (1981), in *Rose, pp.53–69.
Ridley, F., 'The State of Chaucer Studies: A Brief Survey', *Studies in the Age of Chaucer*, I (1979) 3–16.

Source Study

Benson, L. D., and Andersson, T. M., *The Literary Context of Chaucer's Fabliaux* (Indianapolis and New York, 1971).
Bryan, W. F., and Dempster, G. (eds), *Sources and Analogues of Chaucer's Canterbury Tales* (Chicago, 1941).
Fleming, J.V., 'Daun Piers and Dom Pier', *Chaucer Review*, XV (1980–1) 287–94.
Fyler, J. M., *Chaucer and Ovid* (New Haven, Conn., 1979).
Havely, N. R., *Chaucer's Boccaccio* (Cambridge and Totowa, NJ, 1980).
Hoffman, R. L., *Ovid and the Canterbury Tales* (Philadelphia and London, 1966).
Kellogg, A. L., 'The Evolution of the *Clerk's Tale*' (1972), in *Kellogg, pp.276–329.
Miller, R. P., *Chaucer: Sources and Backgrounds* (London and New York, 1977).
Minnis, A., *Chaucer and Pagan Antiquity* (Cambridge and Totowa, NJ, 1982).
Pratt, R. A., 'Chaucer's Claudian', *Speculum*, XXII (1947) 419–29.

'Chaucer and the Hand that Fed Him', *Speculum*, XLI (1966) 619–42.

Salter, E., 'Chaucer and Boccaccio: *The Knight's Tale*', in her *Fourteenth-Century English Poetry* (Oxford, 1983) pp. 141–81.

Schless, H., 'Transformations: Chaucer's Use of Italian' (1974), in *Brewer (1974), pp. 184–223.

Webb, H., 'A Reinterpretation of Chaucer's Theseus', *Review of English Studies*, XXIII (1947) 289–96.

Windeatt, B. A., (ed.), *Geoffrey Chaucer: Troilus and Criseyde* (London and New York, 1984).

Retrieving literary conventions

Brewer, D. S., 'The Ideal of Feminine Beauty in Medieval Literature' (1955), in *Brewer (1982), pp. 30–45.

Burrow, J. A., *Ricardian Poetry* (London and New Haven, (Conn., 1971).

Kean, P. M., *Chaucer and the Making of English Poetry*, vol. II: *The Art of Narrative* (London, 1972).

Lewis, C. S., *The Allegory of Love: A Study in Medieval Tradition* (Oxford, 1936).

Mann, J., *Chaucer and Medieval Estates Satire* (Cambridge, 1973).

Murphy, J. J., *Three Medieval Rhetorical Arts* (Berkeley, Calif., and London, 1971).

Muscatine, C., *Chaucer and the French Tradition* (Berkeley, Calif., 1957).

Payne, R. O., *The Key of Remembrance: A Study of Chaucer's Poetics* (New Haven, Conn., and London, 1963).

Pearcy, R., 'Chaucer's Franklin and the Literary Vavasour', *Chaucer Review*, VIII (1973–4) 33–59.

Medieval intellectual contexts

Curry, W. C., *Chaucer and the Medieval Sciences*, 2nd edn (New York, 1960).

Donaldson, E. T., 'Patristic Exegesis in the Criticism of Medieval Literature: The Opposition' (1960), in *Donaldson, pp. 134–53.

Gaylord, A., 'The Promises in *The Franklin's Tale*', *Journal of English Literary History*, XXXI (1964) 331–65.

Huppé, B., *A Reading of the Canterbury Tales* (Albany, NY, 1964).

Jordan, R., *Chaucer and the Shape of Creation* (Cambridge, Mass., 1967).

Kolve, V. A., *Chaucer and the Imagery of Narrative: The First Five Canterbury Tales* (London, 1984).

Manzalaoui, M., 'Chaucer and Science' (1974), in *Brewer (1974), pp. 224–61.

Miller, R. P., 'Chaucer's Pardoner, the Scriptural Eunuch, and the Pardoner's Tale', *Speculum*, XXX (1955) 180–99.

Roberston, D. W., *A Preface to Chaucer* (Princeton, NJ, 1962).
   'Chaucer's Franklin and his Tale' (1974), in his *Essays in Medieval Culture* (Princeton, NJ, 1980) pp. 273–90.

Rogers, W., 'The Raven and the Writing Desk: The Theoretical Limits of Patristic Criticism', *Chaucer Review*, XIV (1979–80) 260–77.

Wood, C., 'Chaucer and Astrology', in *Rowland, pp. 202–20.

Social and political historicism

Aers, D., *Chaucer, Langland and the Creative Imagination* (London, 1980).

Blamires, A. G., 'Chaucer's Revaluation of Chivalric Honour', *Mediaevalia*, V (1979) 245–69.

Blenner-Hassett, R., 'Autobiographical Aspects of Chaucer's Franklin', *Speculum*, XXVIII (1953) 791–800.

Bowden, M., *A Commentary on the General Prologue to the Canterbury Tales*, 2nd edn (New York and London, 1967).

Brewer, D. S., 'Class-Distinction in Chaucer' (1968), in *Brewer (1982), pp. 54–72.

Coleman, J., *English Literature in History 1350–1400: Medieval Readers and Writers* (London, 1981).

Crow, M. M., and Olson, C. C., *Chaucer Life-Records* (Oxford, 1966).

Diamond, A., 'Chaucer's Women and Women's Chaucer', in *The Authority of Experience: Essays in Feminist Criticism*, ed. A. Diamond and L. R. Edwards (Amherst, Mass., 1977) pp. 60–83.

Du Boulay, F. R. H., 'The Historical Chaucer', in *Brewer (1974), pp. 33–57.

Hamilton, M. P., 'The Credentials of Chaucer's Pardoner', *Journal of English and Germanic Philology*, XL (1941) 48–72.

Haskell, A. S., 'The Portrayal of Women by Chaucer and his

Age', in *What Manner of Woman*, ed M. Springer (New York, 1978) pp. 1–14.

Hotson, J. L., 'Colfox *vs.* Chauntecleer' (1924), in *Wagenknecht, pp. 98–116.

Keen, M., 'Chaucer's Knight, the English Aristocracy, and the Crusade', in *English Court Culture in the Later Middle Ages*, ed V. J. Scattergood (London, 1983).

Kellogg, A., and Haselmayer, L., 'Chaucer's Satire and the Pardoner' (1951) in *Kellogg, pp. 212–44.

Knight, S., 'Chaucer and the Sociology of Literature', *Studies in the Age of Chaucer*, II (1980) 15–51.

Manly, J. M., *Some New Light on Chaucer* (London, 1926).

Muscatine, C., *Poetry and Crisis in the Age of Chaucer* (Notre Dame, Ind., and London, 1972).

Power, E., 'Madame Eglentyne, Chaucer's Prioress in Real Life', in her *Medieval People* (Boston, Mass., 1924) pp. 59–84.

Robertson, S., 'Elements of Realism in the *Knight's Tale*', *Journal of English and Germanic Philology*, XIV (1915) 226–55.

Strohm, P., 'Form and Social Statement in *Confessio Amantis* and *The Canterbury Tales*', *Studies in the Age of Chaucer*, I (1979) 17–40.

Dramatic or psychological readings

Burlin, R., 'The Art of Chaucer's Franklin' (1967), in *Anderson, *Casebook*, pp. 183–208.

Holland, N., 'Meaning as Transformation: The *Wife of Bath's Tale*', *College English*, XXVIII (1967) 279–90.

Jordan, R. M., 'Chaucer's Sense of Illusion: Roadside Drama Reconsidered', *Journal of English and Germanic Philology*, XXIX (1962) 19–33.

Kittredge, G. L., 'Chaucer's Discussion of Marriage' (1912), in *Anderson, *Casebook*, pp. 61–92.

Chaucer and his Poetry (Cambridge, Mass., 1915).

Leicester, H. M., 'The Art of Impersonation: A General Prologue to the *Canterbury Tales*', *Publications of the Modern Language Association*, XCV (1980) 213–24.

Lumiansky, R. M., *Of Sondry Folk: The Dramatic Principle in the Canterbury Tales* (Austin, 1955).

Slade, A., 'Irony in the Wife of Bath's Tale' (1969), in *Anderson, *Casebook*, pp. 172–82.

Varities of textual analysis

Bishop, I., 'The Narrative Art of the Pardoner's Tale' (1967), in *Anderson, *Casebook*, pp. 209–21.

Blake, N. F., *The English Language in Medieval Literature* (London, 1977).

Brewer, D. S., 'Some Metonymic Relationships in Chaucer's Poetry' (1974), in *Brewer (1984), pp. 37–53.
'The Nun's Priest's Tale* as Story and Poem' (1979), in *Brewer (1984), pp. 90–106.

Bronson, B. H., *In Search of Chaucer* (Toronto, 1960).

Burnley, J. D., *Chaucer's Language and the Philosophers' Tradition* (Cambridge and Totowa, NJ, 1979).
A Guide to Chaucer's Language (London, 1983).

Cooper, H., *The Structure of the Canterbury Tales* (London, 1983).

Davis, N., *A Chaucer Glossary* (Oxford, 1979).

Donaldson, E. T., 'Idiom of Popular Poetry in the Miller's Tale' (1950), in *Anderson, *Casebook*, pp. 143–60.
'Chaucer the Pilgrim' (1954), in *Anderson, *Casebook*, pp. 93–104.
'The Manuscripts of Chaucer's Works and their Use', in *Brewer (1974), pp. 85–108.

Frost, W., 'An Interpretation of Chaucer's Knight's Tale' (1949), in *Anderson, *Casebook*, pp. 121–42.

Hoffman, A. W., 'Chaucer's Prologue to Pilgrimage: The Two Voices' (1954), in *Anderson, *Casebook*, pp. 105–20.

Howard, D. R., *The Idea of the Canterbury Tales* (Berkeley, Calif., and London, 1976).

Knight, S., *Rymyng Craftily: Meaning in Chaucer's Poetry* (Sydney and London, 1973).

Mann, J., 'Chaucerian Themes and Style in the *Franklin's Tale*', in *The New Pelican Guide to English Literature*, ed B. Ford, I (Harmondsworth, 1982) pp. 133–53.

Owen, C., 'The Crucial Passages in Five of the *Canterbury Tales*' (1953), in *Wagenknecht, pp. 251–70.
Pilgrimage and Storytelling in the Canterbury Tales (Norman, Okla, 1977).

Pearsall, D. A., '*The Canterbury Tales*', in *Sphere History of Literature in the English Language*, I, ed. W. F. Bolton (London, 1970) pp. 163–94.

Richardson, J., *Blameth Nat Me: A Study of Imagery in Chaucer's*

Fabliaux (The Hague, 1970).

Ross, T. W., *Chaucer's Bawdy* (New York, 1972).

Ruggiers, P. G. (ed.), *The Canterbury Tales: A Facsimile and Transcription of the Hengwrt Manuscript* (Norman, Okla, 1979).

Shoaf, R. A., *Dante, Chaucer, and the Currency of the Word* (Norman, Okla, 1983).

Spearing, A. C., *Criticism and Medieval Poetry*, 2nd edn (London, 1972).

——— (ed.), *The Franklin's Prologue and Tale* (Cambridge, 1966). 'Chaucerian Authority and Inheritance', in *Literature in Fourteenth-Century England*, ed P. Boitani and A. Torti (Tübingen and Cambridge, 1983) pp. 185-202

Whittock, T., *A Reading of the Canterbury Tales* (Cambridge, 1968).

Further reading

Burlin, R. B., *Chaucerian Fiction* (Princeton, 1977).

David, A., *The Strumpet Muse: Art and Morals in Chaucer's Poetry* (Bloomington and London, 1976).

Kane, G., *Chaucer* (Oxford, 1984).

Lawler, T., *The One and the Many in the Canterbury Tales* (Hamden, Connecticut, 1980).

Pearsall, D., *The Canterbury Tales* (London, 1985).

Ruggiers, P.G., *The Art of the Canterbury Tales* (Madison, 1965).

Traversi, D., *The Canterbury Tales: A Reading* (London, 1983).

Medieval sources

Listed in order of citation.

Hoccleve, 'Address to Sir John Oldcastle': *Hoccleve's Works, The Minor Poems*, ed F. J. Furnivall and I. Gollancz, Early English Text Society (1892).

Sir Gawain and the Green Knight, ed J. R. R. Tolkien and E. V. Gordon, rev. N. Davis (Oxford, 1967).

The Book of Margery Kempe, ed. S. B. Meech and H. E. Allen, Early English Text Society (1940).

Boccaccio: The Decameron, transl. G. H. McWilliam (Harmondsworth, 1972).

Fable of the man and the lion: *Caxton's Aesop,* ed. R. T. Lenaghan (Cambridge, Mass., 1967) pp. 132–3.

The Cloud of Unknowing, ed. P. Hodgson, Early English Text Society (1944).

Index to Critics

Index to
Tale-citations